Nuclear Politics and the Non-Aligned Movement: Principles vs Pragmatism

William Potter and Gaukhar Mukhatzhanova

Nuclear Politics and the Non-Aligned Movement: Principles vs Pragmatism

William Potter and Gaukhar Mukhatzhanova

IISS The International Institute for Strategic Studies

The International Institute for Strategic Studies

Arundel House I 13–15 Arundel Street I Temple Place I London I WC2R 3DX I UK

First published February 2012 by **Routledge**
4 Park Square, Milton Park, Abingdon, Oxon, OX14 4RN

for **The International Institute for Strategic Studies**
Arundel House, 13–15 Arundel Street, Temple Place, London, WC2R 3DX, UK
www.iiss.org

Simultaneously published in the USA and Canada by **Routledge**
270 Madison Ave., New York, NY 10016

Routledge is an imprint of Taylor & Francis, an Informa Business

© 2012 The International Institute for Strategic Studies

DIRECTOR-GENERAL AND CHIEF EXECUTIVE Dr John Chipman
EDITOR Dr Nicholas Redman
ASSISTANT EDITOR Janis Lee
EDITORIAL Carolyn West, Dr Jeffrey Mazo, Dr Ayse Abdullah
COVER/PRODUCTION John Buck

The International Institute for Strategic Studies is an independent centre for research, information and debate on the problems of conflict, however caused, that have, or potentially have, an important military content. The Council and Staff of the Institute are international and its membership is drawn from almost 100 countries. The Institute is independent and it alone decides what activities to conduct. It owes no allegiance to any government, any group of governments or any political or other organisation. The IISS stresses rigorous research with a forward-looking policy orientation and places particular emphasis on bringing new perspectives to the strategic debate.

The Institute's publications are designed to meet the needs of a wider audience than its own membership and are available on subscription, by mail order and in good bookshops. Further details at www.iiss.org.

British Library Cataloguing in Publication Data
A catalogue record for this book is available from the British Library

Library of Congress Cataloging in Publication Data

ADELPHI series
ISSN 1944-5571

ADELPHI 427
ISBN 978-0-415-69641-8

Contents

ACKNOWLEDGEMENTS

This book has been a long time in gestation and, as a consequence, owes its current shape to many individuals. First and foremost, the authors wish to express their gratitude to numerous and very gifted diplomats from the Non-Aligned Movement (NAM), who shared their time and insights with us over many years. William Potter is particularly indebted to several dozen busy government diplomats and international organisation officials who met with him in Vienna in July and August 2011. Although they may not all agree fully with the authors' interpretations, collectively their input improved the manuscript immeasurably.

The authors also are very grateful to the exceptional team of past and present experts and visiting scholars from the Center for Nonproliferation Studies who conducted research and contributed material to an unpublished collection of essays on NAM's nuclear politics. They include Patricia Lewis, Sverre Lodgaard, Aruni Wijewardane, Kenley Butler, Sean Dunlop, Vasileios Savvidis and Liviu Horovitz. Support for that research project was provided by the William and Flora Hewlett Foundation, Carnegie Corporation of New York, and the governments of Norway and the United Kingdom. A grant from the Hewlett Foundation made possible the preparation of this manuscript.

It is never an easy task to compress one's arguments into a concise and cogent narrative. To the extent that we succeeded in doing so in this book, it is due in no small measure to the exceptional editorial assistance provided by Emily Johnson. Her contribution is greatly appreciated.

This book only scratches the surface of a subject in need of far more scholarly examination and diplomatic reflection. Hopefully, it will stimulate new research, provoke a lively debate among practitioners and provide both communities with an improved understanding of the policies and politics of the Non-Aligned Movement. If it does so, we will have achieved our major objective.

AP	Additional Protocol to the Comprehensive Safeguards Agreement
BoG	Board of Governors
CTBT	Comprehensive Nuclear Test-Ban Treaty
DPRK	Democratic People's Republic of Korea (North Korea)
ENDC	Eighteen-Nation Disarmament Committee
FMCT	Fissile Material Cut-off Treaty
G-77	The Group of 77
GC	General Conference
HEU	highly enriched uranium
IAEA	International Atomic Energy Agency
INC	Israeli Nuclear Capabilities
INFCIRC	Information Circular (distributed by International Atomic Energy Agency)
LEU	low-enriched uranium
MNA	multilateral nuclear fuel approaches
NAC	New Agenda Coalition
NAM	Non-Aligned Movement
NNWS	non-nuclear-weapons states
NPT	Treaty on the Non-proliferation of Nuclear Weapons
NSG	Nuclear Suppliers Group
NWC	Nuclear Weapons Convention
NWFZ	Nuclear-Weapon-Free Zone
NWS	nuclear-weapons states
Prep Com	Preparatory Committee (of the Treaty on the Non-proliferation of Nuclear Weapons)

Rev Con	Review Conference (of the Treaty on the Non-proliferation of Nuclear Weapons)
TCF	Technical Cooperation Fund
WMD	weapons of mass destruction
UNGA	United Nations General Assembly
UNMOVIC	United Nations Monitoring, Verification and Inspection Commission
UNSC	United Nations Security Council
UNSCR	United Nations Security Council Resolution

INTRODUCTION

The Non-Aligned Movement (NAM) is the world's largest political grouping of states engaged on issues related to international
security.[1] It consists of 120 full members and 17 observer states –
more than two-thirds of the membership of the United Nations.
By virtue of its size alone, the movement has the potential to be a
very constructive or obstructive force in dealing with many of the
most pressing nuclear disarmament, non-proliferation, terrorism
and peaceful-use challenges of the day. These threats include the
continued possession of thousands of nuclear weapons by a small
but growing number of states; the nuclear-weapons ambitions of
additional states; and the possibility that non-state actors may
gain access to fissile material for the purpose of making nuclear
explosives. Additionally, significant nuclear challenges pertain
to the anticipated expansion of peaceful nuclear activities glob-
ally (notwithstanding the economic and political repercussions
from the nuclear disaster at Fukushima in March 2011), the less
than robust nature of the international non-proliferation regime
and the weakening of some of its key components, as well as the
persistence of severe regional security threats and arms races that
could spiral out of control.

Surprisingly, in light of the size and significance of NAM, few Western governments, scholars or non-governmental analysts display much familiarity with NAM politics or perspectives, and there has been a failure to appreciate the diversity of NAM views or the potential for engaging NAM members as partners in various initiatives to mitigate nuclear threats. To the extent that expertise and scholarship exist, they tend to be focused on a very small subset of NAM members, usually regional in nature, and divorced from first-hand experience involving participation in NAM politics or international negotiations with NAM members.[2]

These shortcomings can be addressed, in part, by drawing upon both the direct experience of the authors as delegates from NAM observer states in negotiations involving the Treaty on the Non-proliferation of Nuclear Weapons (NPT) Review Process, as well as participation by one of the authors in several NAM brainstorming meetings convened in advance of NPT Preparatory Committee sessions. These insights have been supplemented by extensive interviews with over two dozen NAM diplomats from Africa, Asia, Latin America and the Middle East, input from senior officials at the United Nations in New York and the International Atomic Energy Agency (IAEA) and Comprehensive Test-Ban Treaty Organisation in Vienna, and from analysis provided by a larger team of researchers at the James Martin Center for Nonproliferation Studies (CNS) at the Monterey Institute of International Studies.[3]

Why NAM matters

The sheer size of NAM vis-à-vis other political groupings in the nuclear arms-control arena makes it a formidable player, whose interests and preferences can only be ignored at great peril. Although size is very much a mixed blessing, contributing to NAM's often plodding decision-making style and an inability to quickly revise positions, it also affords great bargaining – and blocking – power. For example, were a vote to be taken at an NPT Review Conference (Rev Con) and were NAM to vote as a bloc, it would overwhelm all other political groupings, as its membership constitutes nearly three-quarters of the adherents to the NPT.[4] Although the issue of adopting the Additional Protocol as the verification standard for non-nuclear-weapon states has never been brought to a vote, NAM's opposition to this can be cited as the primary reason why neither an NPT Rev Con nor an IAEA General Conference has yet endorsed the proposal. NAM can use its size to influence the international agenda: it is largely responsible for the continuing attention given at international forums to the issue of peaceful nuclear use and various disarmament measures, including nuclear-weapon-free zones. Its large and diverse membership also leads to a phenomenon whereby the collective is often less ready to compromise than its individual members, a characteristic inadequately appreciated by many outside analysts who exaggerate the homogeneity of the movement.

Size alone, however, fails to explain the impact of NAM and the constraints it imposes on the ability of the international community to respond swiftly and effectively to important nuclear-proliferation challenges. As most NAM members have little interest in or expertise on highly technical nuclear matters and possess little institutional capacity to engage effectively in nuclear negotiations, a small number of NAM states can disproportionately influence NAM positions on these issues. These same states tend to have vested interests in the nuclear sphere and hold more extreme positions on crucial nuclear issues than the majority of NAM members. They are thus in a position to shape NAM policy, which they frequently do, notwithstanding a decision-making process within the movement that emphasises consensus.[5]

Although NAM's size, its diversity and its consensus mode of decision-making are not conducive to innovation or adaptability, over the past 50 years NAM has periodically altered its priorities, if not its core principles. It has also exploited periods of Western – and especially US – indifference, ignorance and unilateralism to enhance its impact on global politics, including those related to nuclear matters. For example, given NAM's origins during the height of the Cold War, its aversion to East–West ideological confrontation, and its championship of decolonisation, economic development and nuclear disarmament, one might have expected the movement's demise by the beginning of the twenty-first century. The end of the Cold War, the disappearance of the East–West bloc structure, and the increasing economic clout of many developing countries all appeared to render NAM obsolete. Although NAM's influence initially waned and its members' attention shifted from political to economic issues, a period of US hegemony and unilateralism, ironically, had the effect of breathing new life into the movement, while also radicalising some aspects of its ideology and re-orienting its politics.[6] During this time, NAM members never abandoned their focus on nuclear disarmament, but the debate within the movement on disarmament stagnated as greater emphasis was given to issues related to peaceful nuclear use and regional security, especially in the Middle East. In some respects, this evolution in NAM perspectives reflects a more pragmatic approach to new international circumstances; however, it also represents the ability of some members to impose their preferred principles as policy priorities for the larger collective.

Illustrative of these competing tendencies of principle and pragmatism — and the importance of better understanding the potential power of NAM as a force for both positive and negative change in nuclear affairs — is the process and product of month-long negotiations in New York at the May 2010 NPT Rev Con. NAM came to the conference with both a general working paper outlining its priorities and proposals with respect to the three pillars of the treaty (disarmament, non-proliferation and peaceful use) and another, more focused one devoted to a disarmament action plan with ambitious goals and demands for complete nuclear disarmament by 2025.[7]

Throughout the Rev Con, the movement insisted that the conference adopt strong, forward-looking language from its working papers, appearing to signal that a compromise on a more modest disarmament action plan was out of the question. Constituting more than two-thirds of the conference participants, representatives of NAM frequently made reference during debates in plenary and working group meetings to their numerical advantage and the need for the Rev Con to reflect the movement's interests. And yet, the repeated references by NAM members to their combined size were probably more indicative of frustration and weakness than strength, as no one – least of all those within the movement – really expected or wanted decisions to be taken by a vote. Ultimately, NAM members supported a consensus final document that served the particular interests of Egypt – the NAM chair – and a number of other states from the Middle East, even though many other NAM states were critical of the document's provisions relating to nuclear disarmament. The result, in other words, reflected NAM's ability to exert considerable leverage when its members toed a common line and when they were prepared to adopt what most of the international community perceived to be a pragmatic approach that advanced the overall well-being of the non-proliferation regime.

Similar pragmatism and flexibility were evident in the positions of some key NAM members in the lead-up to and conclusion of the April 2010 Nuclear Security Summit in

Washington. The Conference Communiqué and Work Plan agreed to by leaders from 47 states included language on the need to minimise the use of highly enriched uranium (HEU) in the civilian nuclear sector as a means to combat nuclear terrorism. Although two leading members of NAM – South Africa and Egypt – had expressed reservations about this initiative as an encroachment on their 'inalienable right' to peaceful nuclear use since the measure was first introduced at the 2005 NPT Rev Con, most NAM members had no interest in the topic because they possessed no HEU. In the absence of a formal NAM position on HEU minimisation and given that Iran had not been invited to the summit, South Africa and Egypt acquiesced to the US- and Norwegian-led HEU initiative once language was added that made minimisation conditional on its technical and economic feasibility – caveats that were preferred by several Western states. Although a number of more ideologically inclined NAM members, including Belarus, Cuba, Iran and Venezuela, attempted to have NAM issue a condemnation of the Washington Summit in advance of the meeting, Egypt as chair of NAM was dismissive of the initiative and, along with a number of other NAM members, indicated its intent to participate in its national capacity.

A very different scenario played out at the September 2010 IAEA General Conference, where principles overshadowed pragmatism on the part of many NAM members and, arguably, also on the part of the United States. The debate revolved around the wisdom of re-introducing a resolution on Israeli nuclear capabilities whose narrow adoption at the 2009 General Conference had deeply divided the assembled delegations and was one of the most bitterly contested battles at the IAEA in memory.[8] Although several NAM members, including South Africa and the Philippines, were worried that a new debate on the issue might impede prospects for implementing the 2010 NPT Rev Con recommendations on the Middle East, the Arab Group – with support from Iran and Cuba – insisted on the introduction of the resolution despite vocal opposition by the United States. (The US asserted that if the resolution were introduced, it would not only be defeated, but would greatly diminish the likelihood that Israel would participate in the NPT Rev Con-mandated Conference on the Middle East, scheduled to take place in the latter half of 2012.[9]) The United States' basic forecast proved correct, and the resolution was soundly defeated, an indication of how the West under certain circumstances can peel votes away from NAM, in this instance largely from among African members for whom Middle Eastern issues were not a high priority. The US success in this instance, however, was achieved at considerable cost and fostered a great deal of bad blood among more moderate NAM countries. This latter group might well have been prepared to strike a compromise had the United States indicated greater readiness to listen to them. Instead, US representatives tended to respond to the strident statements made by more ideological and extreme members, leading to the contraction of space for constructive dialogue.

International negotiations at the 2010 NPT Rev Con and similar deliberations at the IAEA Board of Governors and General Conference over issues of nuclear-fuel assurances, the nuclear activities of Iran and Israel, and nuclear security illustrate the impact that NAM has on major non-proliferation and nuclear-terrorism issues and the potential for the movement to be both a major constructive and obstructive force. They also demonstrate why a keen understanding of NAM nuclear policies and perspectives is vital to finding mutually acceptable solutions to some of the most vexing and important challenges of our time.

CHAPTER ONE

NAM origins, structure, policymaking and politics

From Brioni[1] hope has come to mankind
Hope and justice for all men as one kind
Tito, Nehru, Nasser gave us piece of mind
When they built the movement of the Non-Aligned.

*'Song of the Non-Aligned World', title song
of an album released in Belgrade in 1987*[2]

Origins

The Non-Aligned Movement (NAM) was formally founded in September 1961 in Belgrade, Yugoslavia, during a conference of 25 heads of state or government from developing countries. The origins of NAM, however, can be traced back to the late 1940s, and can be viewed as a reaction by many developing nations to the growth of Cold War blocs and ideological rivalries following the end of the Second World War. A number of these countries had only recently liberated themselves from colonial rule, and they were anxious to avoid new entanglements.

Most notable among the leaders of this emergent grouping of states were Yugoslavia's Josip Broz Tito, who was intent on avoiding the yoke of Soviet imperialism, and India's Jawaharlal Nehru, who was a principal leader of his country's successful struggle to gain independence from the United Kingdom. Also prominent in the emergence of the Non-Aligned Movement and the development of its initial political orientation were Egypt's Gamel Nasser, Indonesia's Sukarno and Ghana's Kwame Nkrumah. Although these figures were very different personalities from diverse economic and political backgrounds, they shared a common aversion to East–West ideological confrontation and championed economic development, liberation from colonialism and nuclear disarmament.[3]

An important event in the development and crystallisation of NAM was a meeting of 29 Asian and African states in Bandung, Indonesia, in April 1955, six years before the Belgrade conference. The Bandung Conference condemned 'colonialism in all of its manifestations' – an implicit censure of both Western and Soviet behaviour – and adopted ten principles on 'promotion of world peace and cooperation', which subsequently figured prominently in NAM goals and perspectives. These were:

1. Respect for fundamental human rights and the objectives of the Charter of the United Nations;

2. Respect for the sovereignty and territorial integrity of all nations;

3. Recognition of equality among all races and the equality among all nations, large and small;

4. Non-intervention and non-interference in the internal affairs of another country;

5. Respect for the right of every nation to defend itself, either individually or collectively;

6. (a) Non-use of collective defence pacts to benefit the specific interests of any of the great powers;
   (b) Non-use of pressure by any country against other countries;

7. Refraining from acts or threats of aggression, or the use of force against the territorial integrity or political independence of any country;

8. Peaceful resolution of all international conflicts in conformity with the Charter of the United Nations;

9. Promotion of mutual interests and cooperation; and

10. Respect for justice and international obligations.[4]

Many of these points were reiterated, albeit in somewhat different language, in the Havana Declaration of September 1979, on the occasion of the sixth summit of heads of state or government from non-aligned countries. This declaration of NAM, which by then had grown to 95 members, identified several dozen 'essential objectives' of the movement, including 'ending the arms race and the achievement of general and complete disarmament under effective international control'.[5] As will be discussed in more detail in a subsequent chapter, the Havana Summit and the three-year period in the late 1970s when Cuba chaired NAM are also illustrative of the potential for and constraints on more ideologically oriented members hijacking the movement for their own national purposes.

The end of the Cold War, the collapse of the Soviet Union and the diminished nature of East–West superpower rivalry in the early 1990s might have been expected to lead to the disappearance of NAM, or at least the change of its name, which appeared to be anachronistic following the dismantling of the Eastern bloc. Although some consideration was given to modifying the group's name, with Egypt reportedly proposing a merger of NAM and the G-77, these ideas gained little traction. Instead, what transpired was a great deal of soul searching by some members, a growing divergence of views within NAM, a period of diminished influence by the movement on global politics and, over time, a re-orientation of NAM priorities.[6]

As Ednan Agaev and Sergei Krylov note, a reassessment of
the role and position of the movement in international politics began as early as 1989, during the ninth NAM Summit in
Belgrade.[7] The text of the Belgrade Declaration directly recognised that the world was at a crossroads, acknowledged the
improved global political climate, and applauded the embarka-
tion by the Soviet Union and the United States 'upon the path
of reducing their huge military arsenals and armed forces'. The
resulting détente provided 'a window of opportunity for the
international community' – developments for which NAM,
according to the Belgrade document, deserved credit.[8]

This re-examination intensified in the early 1990s at a time
when Yugoslavia – one of the founders of NAM and its past
elected chair – disintegrated, Argentina withdrew from the
movement and Iraq (a NAM member) attacked another NAM
member, Kuwait. During this period of sweeping changes
in the post-Cold War international system and the widely
perceived reduction in the risk of traditional nuclear dangers,
it was natural for NAM also to increase the priority it attached
to economic and developmental – as opposed to international
security – issues. At the same time, NAM found itself increasingly isolated at multilateral forums, where it had previously
enjoyed the frequent support of the Soviet Union and its allies.
During the last decade of the twentieth century, a number of
NAM states had developed closer economic and political relationships with the United States, and in some instances also
had forged military cooperation and strategic ties with the
dominant superpower. This reorientation was by no means
an indication that NAM had, as a collective, abandoned its
long-standing interest in and commitment to the principle of
nuclear disarmament. Indeed, as discussed in more detail in
the next chapter, a number of members played crucial roles in
making possible the indefinite extension of the NPT in 1995

and the adoption of major disarmament and non-proliferation measures at the 2000 NPT Review Conference. Nevertheless, NAM found it increasingly difficult in the 1990s to stake out a strong, distinctive and coherent position on nuclear disarmament at a time when two of its members – India and Pakistan – chose to demonstrate their own nuclear-weapons prowess by conducting a series of nuclear-weapons tests.

Ironically, it was the emergence of US hegemony and the rejection of multilateralism by the George W. Bush administration that provided a new *raison d'être* and life-line for the Non-Aligned Movement in the sphere of nuclear disarmament. While many NAM members could appreciate why the United States was concerned about the risk of nuclear terrorism in the wake of 11 September 2001, they tended to be unsympathetic to Washington's preoccupation with that danger, along with its fixation on regime change of three NAM members (the so-called 'axis of evil'), to the neglect of multilateral disarmament initiatives. Although NAM was not alone in its criticism of the behaviour of the only remaining superpower, the confrontation with the United States over its embrace of unilateralism and 'coalitions of the willing' enabled the movement to regain its voice and purpose on nuclear issues. It also facilitated the rise in influence within NAM of several more ideologically inclined members who possessed national agendas that were very much at odds with US interests.

Structure and decision-making

NAM's newest members – Azerbaijan and Fiji – were admitted in May 2011, bringing the group's membership to 120 full members and 17 observer countries.[9] (See Appendix I for a full list).

Although the movement is often depicted by outside analysts as a homogenous group of developing states, in many respects

NAM is and has always been a diverse coalition. While predominantly non-nuclear adherents to the NPT, NAM members and observers include three nuclear-weapons states (India, Pakistan and the Democratic People's Republic of Korea), one country that developed an indigenous nuclear-weapons capability but then dismantled it (South Africa), and three other states (Belarus, Kazakhstan and Ukraine) that possessed nuclear weapons on their territory but chose to remove them and join the NPT as non-nuclear-weapons states. NAM also contains countries ranging in economic development from among the poorest in the world, such as Yemen, Somalia and Myanmar, to some of the wealthiest, such as Singapore, the United Arab Emirates and Qatar. In addition, NAM members vary significantly in their form of government, religious faith and regional distribution (although only one NAM member – Belarus – is located in Europe).

Although it is a large and diverse political grouping, the Non-Aligned Movement has a fairly loose and informal organisational structure, which makes it more difficult for outside observers to discern its political dynamics, foreign-policy positions and decision-making processes. NAM has no charter, permanent secretariat or headquarters, or, for that matter, a permanent website. The most recent information regarding NAM policy tends to be posted on the website of the host of the last NAM Summit for Heads of State/Government, in this instance that of the Sharm el-Sheikh Summit in Egypt in July 2009.[10]

NAM practice is for the group to take all decisions by consensus. In the NAM context, however, the definition of 'consensus' is a liberal one that does not connote unanimity. Rather, it implies a strong convergence of views, a formula that accommodates the diversity of NAM and enables members to express 'general reservations' about a particular issue on which they vote in the minority, without calling into question the overall orientation of the group. This practice allows states to occasionally articulate national positions on subjects of particular importance to them that diverge from the NAM majority position, while maintaining good standing within the movement. It also is a practice that any NAM chair must bear in mind, as it provides a vehicle for members to express their discontent should the chair (or another particularly vocal state or group of states) attempt to act arbitrarily or otherwise impose positions that diverge from established NAM norms.

Although NAM may lack many of the formal structures that characterise most institutions, it maintains a number of institutional arrangements, including a chair, a Coordinating Bureau in New York, and a Joint Coordinating Committee to foster cooperation between NAM and the G-77. In fact, as A.W. Singham and Shirley Hune point out in their analysis of NAM's structure and organisation, it has a considerable administrative apparatus, but it is tailored to the peculiar needs of a multicultural, transnational social movement consisting of states with different ideologies and objectives.[11] Although one may question the appropriateness of this original structure in today's very different environment, NAM's structure and decision-making process continue to be guided by the administrative principle – if not always consistent practice – of non-hierarchical, rotational and inclusive participation.

The chair

The country that chairs NAM at any given period of time serves as its temporary secretariat and bears the responsibility of organising relevant meetings and making available the movement's documents, declarations, position papers, and other materials. The chairing state typically creates or designates a section of its ministry of foreign affairs to serve as the 'NAM

Ministry' and Secretariat for the duration of its chairmanship. The position usually rotates every three years on the occasion of the summit of heads of state/government (this practice may vary depending on circumstances – for example, South Africa held chairmanship for more than four years in 1998–2003). A principle of geographical rotation also is supposed to guide the selection process. Theoretically, this arrangement is all-inclusive, non-hierarchical and non-discriminatory, and provides all members with the opportunity to assume the post of chair. In practice, however, the organisational leadership position requires considerable capacity and commitment, with the result that only those states with necessary resources and interests routinely vie for the position.

The 'Troika'

The concept of a NAM Troika – the previous, current and future chair – is a relatively recent organisational innovation in the movement, having emerged in 1997. The current NAM Troika as of late 2011 is comprised of Cuba, Egypt and Iran.

Meetings

The highest decision-making authority in NAM is vested in the Summit Conference of Heads of State or Government, which typically meets every three years and yields, among other documents, a formal negotiated declaration setting out collective NAM positions on a wide variety of issues. The most recent NAM Summit in Sharm el-Sheikh (2009), for example, set forth NAM perspectives on issues such as UN Security Council reform, terrorism, disarmament and international security, the Middle East, human rights and development. The format and proceedings of the meetings are currently guided by the principles outlined in the movement's Cartagena Document on Methodology (1996), which was reaffirmed at the 14th NAM

Summit in Cuba ten years later.[12] (See Appendix II for a list of prior NAM summits.) In addition to summits, NAM also convenes ministerial conferences, which review the work of the movement and issue programmatic documents and position papers when necessary. For example, the 1996 meeting of the ministerial committee on methodology in Cartagena, Colombia, led to the adoption of the Cartagena document on NAM methodology, while the ministerial meeting in Tehran in 2008 produced a statement in support of Iran's nuclear programme. At the most recent ministerial meeting in Jakarta in May 2011, five documents were adopted, including one on nuclear disarmament, two related to Palestine, and a commemoration on the occasion of the movement's 50th anniversary. Additional high-level meetings are held in New York during sessions of the UN General Assembly.

NAM also has a multitude of working groups, task forces and committees on a variety of issues that meet as necessary. They include a Working Group on Disarmament, which routinely is chaired by Indonesia. The Indonesia Mission in New York also periodically convenes weekend brainstorming meetings for NAM diplomats and outside experts on disarmament and non-proliferation matters.[13]

Coordination of activities

In 1973, NAM established a Coordinating Bureau that includes representatives of all member states. It is headed by the permanent representative to the United Nations in New York of the current NAM Chair. The Bureau's role and functions have expanded over time and currently include the review of the activities of working groups, improvement of cooperation among member states, coordination of positions and actions in the UN and other international structures, and drafting of declarations and position papers. The Joint

Coordination Committee of NAM and the G-77 meets in New York as well.

To ensure that the movement's views are represented in a unified manner in the UN Security Council, NAM established a Security Council Caucus, which consists of those states holding non-permanent Security Council seats at a given time. The head of the Caucus and the chair of the Coordinating Bureau are supposed to meet regularly to review Security Council developments and to ensure that the Caucus coordinator is fully apprised of NAM positions.

In principle, the Caucus is supposed to defend NAM positions during Security Council deliberations and ensure that NAM views are reflected in Security Council decisions and documents. In practice, however, NAM member states on the Security Council – like states from other political groupings – tend to act first and foremost in their individual capacity in pursuit of national interests that do not always correspond with the collective NAM positions. The movement therefore often finds it challenging to maintain unified positions among member states on the Security Council. In autumn 2009, for example, this difficulty was pronounced during the negotiation and adoption of the UN Security Council Resolution 1887 on nuclear non-proliferation and disarmament.[14] The chair of the Coordinating Bureau (Egypt) did not have an opportunity to address the Security Council Summit in September 2009, nor did the NAM member states and observers on the Council at the time (Burkina Faso, Costa Rica, Libya, Mexico, Uganda and Vietnam) push in a coordinated or concerted fashion for the incorporation of key NAM positions into the resolution, especially with respect to nuclear disarmament and the Middle East. Instead, NAM had to content itself with sending a letter to the Security Council containing an excerpt from the final summit document adopted the preceding July in Sharm el-Sheikh.

Only after the fact, following the adoption of the resolution by consensus, did the NAM chapter in Vienna protest that the resolution was heavy on non-proliferation and light on disarmament, and therefore should not serve as a basis for any kind of agreement in the NPT context.

NAM activities in Vienna and Geneva

In the disarmament and non-proliferation sphere, additional arrangements are in place to facilitate coordination of NAM positions in Vienna and Geneva. The NAM Vienna Chapter was established in 2003, during Malaysia's chairmanship, for the purpose of enhancing the movement's representation at the IAEA, particularly with respect to issues of nuclear safeguards. Subsequently, NAM also began to meet regularly to prepare statements for conferences and preparatory committee meetings of the Comprehensive Test-Ban Treaty Organisation, also located in Vienna. Because there are fewer NAM members at the IAEA than at the United Nations, the composition of the Vienna Chapter has a different complexion and its actions do not always coincide perfectly with those of the larger NAM collective.[15]

The Vienna Chapter of NAM became particularly active after 2005 due to growing international concerns about Iran's nuclear programme and the very active role of Iran within NAM and at the IAEA. As is the case for the NAM Coordinating Bureau in New York, the NAM Vienna Chapter is led by the ambassador from the country currently serving as chair of NAM. In addition, there is a standing working group at the expert level (below the rank of ambassador) that is always chaired by a representative from the state currently heading NAM. Negotiations over NAM statements to the IAEA Board of Governors and General Conference take place in this forum, which conveys its recommendations to the NAM plenary, usually attended by ambassadors. Recommendations from the working group are typically adopted with little debate at the plenary, which on occasion also may consider additional issues that were not first vetted in the working group.

Although not by design, in some respects the Vienna Chapter has evolved into a counterpart, if not rival, to the New York-based Coordinating Bureau on certain issues of nuclear disarmament, non-proliferation, peaceful use and regional security. In part this development is a natural function of different personalities and priorities at the two venues, as well as the very different competencies of NAM members on issues relevant to the work of the international organisations in New York and Vienna.

Consistent with the general operation of NAM, the Vienna Chapter head is supposed to consult with member states in plenary meetings on major issues leading to a 'NAM consensus'. The outcome of such consultations, however, depends to a large degree on the personalities of the representatives, the level of representation at any plenary, the expertise of the individuals present, and the time available for deliberation. Although the NAM Chapter may strive for unified positions at meetings of the IAEA Board of Governors and the General Conference, in practice there often is a tug-of-war among different leading members that reflect national interests, as well as collective principles and positions, especially on issues where the United States and other nuclear-weapons states (NWS) bring great pressure to bear. As discussed later, recurrent friction over issues such as Iran's compliance with its non-proliferation obligations and Israel's nuclear-weapons capabilities makes it increasingly difficult for NAM to maintain a unified position.

Although at times it can be difficult to distinguish the G-77 from NAM because of a very significant overlap of members, the former also operates out of Vienna, among other venues.

The G-77 established its Vienna Chapter in 1998 in the context of the United Nations Industrial Development Organization (UNIDO). Although playing a far less visible role in the international security sector than NAM, it also engages on a number of related issues having to do with economic and scientific developments, including those in the nuclear sector. For example, the G-77 has been very much involved in recent discussions pertaining to multilateralisation of the nuclear fuel cycle. Although the chairs for NAM and the G-77 are for different durations and do not normally coincide, in January 2011 Iran assumed the chairmanship of the G-77 in Vienna. Its performance there may offer some clues about its behaviour in NAM when it assumes the chairmanship of that group in 2012.

NAM also maintains chapters in Geneva, the Hague and Paris, but they tend to assume a low profile.[16] A large number of NAM members in Geneva are nonetheless active among the so-called Group of 21 (now consisting of 33 countries), which serves as a coordination body for many developing states at the Conference on Disarmament. The Group of 21 often puts forward NAM positions at the Conference on Disarmament, although it is not directly linked to the NAM Coordinating Bureau or other NAM structures.

Opinion leaders and special interests

NAM formally operates on a one-state, one-vote basis. As in all political groupings, however, some NAM members and observers are more influential than others. This influence can stem from a number of factors, including the state's reputation and resources (economic, institutional and otherwise), the importance a country attaches to the movement, the personality, charisma and intellect of individual leaders, and the priority issues for NAM at any particular time. Institutional mechanisms such as the chairmanship of the movement may also be harnessed by states to promote particular issues of national importance that fall within the overall NAM mandate.

As the origins and evolution of NAM illustrate, the leadership and the influence of individual states within NAM has changed dramatically over time. One of its founding members – Yugoslavia – no longer exists; another, India, attaches far less attention and significance to the movement than it once did, having acquired the military and political means to chart a more independent and nationally oriented course in global affairs. The role of another initially influential member, Ghana, rapidly diminished with the passing from the scene of its once powerful leader Kwame Nkrumah. Other latecomers to NAM quickly catapulted their states to leadership roles within the movement, in part due to their personal reputations and those acquired by their countries through struggles to overcome adversity and by demonstration of their commitment to core NAM principles.

Perhaps the best example of the rapid ascension to a leadership role in NAM is South Africa, which joined in 1994 following democratic elections, and four years later hosted the 12th NAM Summit of Heads of State or Government in Durban. As a remarkable success story in both peacefully overcoming apartheid and disbanding an indigenous nuclear-weapons programme, South Africa had exceptional moral authority and credibility for its principled positions both within NAM and internationally. Significantly, it chose to apply that political capital with great effect at the 1995 NPT Review and Extension Conference, where its ideas for strengthening the NPT Review Process and adopting a set of Principles and Objectives for Nuclear Disarmament and Non-Proliferation were instrumental in gaining the indefinite extension of the NPT.[17]

Other countries derive great influence from the expertise they bring to the table. One of the reasons that Iran – as well as

South Africa – is so active and effective within NAM on nuclear matters is its longstanding experience and institutional capacity with respect to nuclear energy, trade and technology. The vast majority of NAM members have little, if any, expertise on these issues and – at least until recently – very limited interest. They are thus in a poor position to challenge the assertions or advance alternative draft language for resolutions on highly technical nuclear matters put forth by very talented diplomats from countries with nuclear know-how, even if they are sceptical about the positions that NAM is being asked to endorse. This expertise can cut in both directions – to promote or obstruct nuclear disarmament and non-proliferation – but it is almost always used in a manner that advances the perceived national interests of the countries with superior technical capacity.

An interesting example of this phenomenon pertains to two very active states within NAM, who are not formal members. Brazil is only a NAM observer, and yet is a powerful voice both within and on behalf of NAM on nuclear technology and trade issues, among others, at the IAEA and in the NPT Review Process. Similarly, Mexico – also a NAM observer – often has effectively championed the Movement's views and positions on nuclear disarmament within the Conference on Disarmament, the United Nations First Committee and the NPT Review Process. These observers on occasion may speak as if they were formal NAM members, but their observer status also allows them greater freedom to part company with NAM when their national positions diverge from those of the collective.[18] An example of such a departure came near the conclusion of the 2009 NPT Preparatory Committee Meeting, when Brazil took exception to the Indonesian statement on behalf of NAM. The Brazilian representative expressed regret that states parties should be so quick to congratulate themselves on adopting an agenda for the 2010 Review Conference while abandoning efforts to agree on any substantive recommendations.

Members of NAM are also inclined to defer to those states and sub-groupings of states on issues that are of greatest importance to those regional parties. This tendency is most apparent with respect to the role of the Arab states on issues associated with Israel and the Middle East. The traditional leader of this regional grouping of states is Egypt, which for many years has made the issue of Israeli adherence to the NPT and the negotiation of a Nuclear-Weapon-Free Zone (NWFZ) in the Middle East the touchstone by which it judged all other disarmament and non-proliferation initiatives, including support for the IAEA Additional Protocol, ratification of the Comprehensive Test-Ban Treaty, signing and ratification of the Convention on the Physical Protection of Nuclear Material, and adherence to the Chemical Weapons Convention.[19] Because of the importance of the issue to Egypt and its long-standing role in promoting the Middle East NWFZ, other NAM members were prepared to give Egypt considerable leeway in its negotiation as Chair of NAM on Middle East issues at the 2010 NPT Review Conference. Once Egypt secured its desired language regarding the Middle East, it refrained from pushing very hard on other aspects of the Conference Final Document relating to nuclear disarmament, even though many NAM members would have preferred much stronger language on that topic.

Interestingly, some members of NAM may achieve influence by virtue of their reputation as 'outlier' states – that is, countries that typically are the least willing to accept NAM positions that are not directly related to core economic and development issues. Chile and Singapore, for example, may be courted (or pressured) by other NAM states on initiatives for which they are seen as pushing against the grain of NAM leadership. Although these outlier countries do not always adopt a single posture, or find themselves in disagreement with the silent majority – on occasion they are joined by other dissenters – they are more inclined than many members to vocalise their disagreements, both publicly and privately. This behaviour can be observed in the debates and votes in Vienna on both substantive and procedural issues related to the nuclear programmes of Iran and Syria; the process by which the Vienna Chapter responded to UN Security Council Resolution 1887; debates during the 2010 NPT Review Conference over the Additional Protocol and Nuclear-Weapon-Free Zone in the Middle East; and skirmishes over the provisions to be contained in the Nuclear Security Summit Communiqué and Work Plan.

One also should note that most members of NAM that belong to the G-77 attach far greater importance to the latter group, because it deals more directly with the 'bread and butter' issues of economic development. Although many of these states are not unsympathetic to the aspirations of more vocal NAM states regarding nuclear disarmament and other international security matters, they are frequently ill-prepared or disinclined to volunteer independent judgements on these topics. As one senior NAM diplomat explained in particularly candid terms, not all NAM members are shining examples of the movement's guiding principles; for some who rarely partake actively in NAM debates, the movement represents a place to be if the alternative is to be politically isolated and out in the cold.[20]

Based on her experience as a Singapore diplomat in Vienna, Yvonne Yew recently proposed an alternative scheme for distinguishing among NAM players: 'leaders', 'spoilers' and 'others'. In the first category, she places countries such as Algeria, Egypt, Malaysia and South Africa, who in the past have served as NAM chairs and benefited by 'identifying closely with NAM principled positions', especially those emphasising development goals and divergent North–South perspectives. NAM spoilers, such as Cuba, Iran, Syria and Venezuela, she suggests, also seize upon the North–South divide and the development credo of NAM, but in pursuit of more individual political agendas cloaked in NAM disguise. She maintains that Iran and Syria attempt to deflect attention from their safeguards transgressions by framing their policies in terms of nuclear rights and peaceful nuclear-use principles.[21] Although useful in highlighting the blocking role played by a small number of very vocal and more ideologically oriented NAM members, Yew's scheme probably understates the leadership capacity of Iran – for good or for bad – while also exaggerating the influence of would-be spoiler states such as Venezuela and Syria, whose strident positions may actually promote a search for common ground by other NAM members.

A more significant conceptual contribution of Yew's, and one that we will make use of in our examination of NAM politics, is to think about the movement in three related but distinct ways – as a normative *concept* based on a set of shared values and goals, as a loose multinational *association* with the kinds of political cleavages and machinations typical of most large political associations, and as a *foreign policy tool* that may be used to promote national objectives that are not always coincident with those of the larger collective.[22]

This simple but profound distinction between different conceptions of the movement – perhaps expanded slightly to conceive of it also as a form of identity[23] – goes a long way towards answering some important questions about NAM. Why has NAM persisted as a political grouping for over five decades despite fundamental changes in the international system and growing diversity within the movement? How have a small number of more ideologically oriented states often been able to significantly influence NAM positions on nuclear issues? Why do formal NAM positions on non-proliferation issues often diverge from national positions taken by NAM members? And what might be done to expand cooperation across political groupings on a variety of nuclear-disarmament, non-proliferation, peaceful use and counter-terrorism issues?

CHAPTER TWO

NAM, nuclear non-proliferation and the 2010 NPT Review Conference

The Treaty on the Non-Proliferation of Nuclear Weapons (NPT) is usually depicted as having three pillars: non-proliferation, disarmament and peaceful use. Nuclear disarmament has always been more central to core NAM principles than non-proliferation. Nevertheless, a number of the movement's members and observers have played important roles in the development of the international non-proliferation regime, including its cornerstone, the NPT. Non-aligned states significantly influenced not only the language of the treaty that entered into force in 1970, but also its indefinite extension in 1995 and the outcome of subsequent five-year NPT Review Conferences, including the most recent one in 2010.

NAM's impact on the NPT can be attributed to a variety of factors, not least of which is sheer numbers. As of mid-2011, all but three of the movement's 120 members were parties to the treaty,[1] out of a total membership of 189 states.[2] To the extent that projected vote counts influence Review Conference decisions, and that NAM is seen as a cohesive bloc, broad approval by its members is a requisite for agreements to be reached. Although a strong preference for consensual decision-making in the NPT Review Process dilutes the numerical influence of NAM somewhat, it still has considerable negotiating power.

NAM's influence over NPT affairs is not only a function of its size. It also stems from the commitment, expertise, ingenuity and negotiating skill of a number of leading NAM members and observers. Countries such as Brazil, Egypt, Mexico, Sri Lanka and South Africa, for example, have at different times in the treaty's history played a major role because of their staunch commitment to disarmament principles, the centrality of the NPT to their national and regional foreign-policy objectives, and the negotiating prowess of individual diplomats. But true to the central principle of 'unity in diversity', from the negotiation of the NPT in the 1960s to the latest Review Conference in 2010, there have been variations among the NAM states' views, priorities and approaches to the treaty, which have often been masked by the 'official' NAM position.

Broadly speaking, the movement remains united in the conviction that the ultimate goal of the NPT is nuclear disarmament. Members differ, however, in their views on how to advance the disarmament goal, their emphasis on other nuclear issues and their positions on measures such as the Additional Protocol. The level and quality of engagement between the NAM and Western states in the context of the NPT has also varied through the years, with much of the first decade of the twenty-first century representing a low point.

In the lead-up to the 2010 NPT Review Conference, it was widely anticipated that the success of the conference would hinge to a large extent on the ability of states parties to make progress on both disarmament issues and implementation of the 1995 Resolution on the Middle East (which called on all Middle Eastern states to accede to the NPT and to establish an effectively verifiable zone free of weapons of mass destruction in the region), a resolution that was central to the agreement to extend the NPT indefinitely in 1995.[3] The Non-Aligned Movement had a major stake in both issues, as nuclear disarmament was a long-standing core principle and goal, and making headway on the Middle East Resolution was a central foreign-policy objective of Egypt – the NAM chair at the time of the 2010 Review Conference – as well as the most cohesive grouping within the NAM, the Arab group. However, in advance of the conference, it was unclear what would constitute sufficient progress on the disarmament front to secure NAM support for a final consensus document.

At the outset of the Review Conference, the movement submitted both a working paper outlining its overall recommendations for conference action and a more narrowly focused paper that proposed an ambitious nuclear-disarmament plan.[4] As Egyptian Ambassador Maged Abdelaziz noted at the close of the conference, NAM's proposals were not adequately reflected in the final text. According to Abdelaziz, 'the outcome had not benefited greatly from the proposals submitted to the Conference by the Group [NAM] in its relevant working papers'.[5] Other NAM members and observers also expressed mixed feelings about the outcome, with representatives of Chile, Cuba, Mexico and South Africa stating that the Final Document 'was far from perfect' or 'fell short of expectations'.[6] Why, then, did NAM as a political grouping accept the final document, and what part did the movement play in its negotiation? In seeking to answer these questions, it will also be relevant to explore the manner in which NAM norms influenced the movement's positions at the Review Conference, the dynamics and process by which NAM decisions were taken on selected issues in a large multilateral negotiating forum, and the way in which some NAM states used the movement's platform to promote national policy preferences. An analysis of NAM negotiating behaviour at the 2010 NPT Review Conference and its mixed record of cooperation and conflict with other political groupings during the month-long nuclear negotiation affords insights into the movement's priorities in the nuclear sphere, as well as the potential for future engagement between NAM and non-NAM states party to the NPT.

NAM and the NPT: the (pre-)history

Unlike nuclear disarmament, non-proliferation was never a central tenet of the Non-Aligned Movement, and on occasion at the height of the Cold War some NAM members even expressed their disenchantment about the degree to which the two nuclear superpowers cooperated on nuclear non-proliferation matters. Although non-proliferation has never been closely entwined with other core NAM precepts, some non-aligned states have, since the initiation of negotiations of the NPT, attached great importance to the issue and have actively sought to shape the content of the treaty and its implementation. The vast majority have also complied consistently with the terms of the treaty, even if they took exception to its discriminatory nature.

As Mohamed Shaker documents in his authoritative history of *The Nuclear Non-Proliferation Treaty: Origins and Implementation, 1959–1979,* one can trace the initial engagement on the NPT by some non-aligned states to the early days of its negotiation at the Eighteen-Nation Disarmament Committee (ENDC). According to Shaker, the ENDC 'played a central part' in NPT negotiations, and its deliberations influenced the formulation of the five principles that served as the basis for the future treaty.[7] These five principles were outlined in UN General Assembly Resolution 2028 (XX), 'Non-Proliferation of Nuclear Weapons', in 1965, on behalf of the eight non-aligned members of the committee: Brazil, Burma, Ethiopia, India, Mexico, Nigeria, Sweden and the United Arab Republic (subsequently Egypt and Syria).[8] The five principles were the following:

(a) The treaty should be void of any loop-holes which might permit nuclear or non-nuclear Powers to proliferate, directly or indirectly, nuclear weapons in any form.

(b) The treaty should embody an acceptable balance of mutual responsibilities and obligations of the nuclear and non-nuclear Powers.

(c) The treaty should be a step towards the achievement of general and complete disarmament and, more particularly, nuclear disarmament.

(d) There should be acceptable and workable provisions to ensure the effectiveness of the treaty.

(e) Nothing in the treaty should adversely affect the right of any group of States to conclude regional treaties in order to ensure the total absence of nuclear weapons in their territories.[9]

As Shaker notes, the resolution and the principles it contained were a product of careful negotiations and compromise not only between 'the Eight' and the two superpowers, but also among the eight non-aligned states themselves, an early indication of the diversity of NAM views on the subject.[10]

The resolution's compromise language was vague, if not weak at times (especially compared to NAM statements and papers today[11]), but the resolution is remarkable in reflecting a high level of engagement between the non-aligned states and the two superpowers at the early stages in the development of what was to become the NPT. The resolution is also indicative of the constructive contribution to the process made by a number of NAM states. Diverse as they were, the eight non-aligned states were able to forge common positions on and interpretations of the principles in the joint memoranda on non-proliferation submitted to the ENDC in 1965 and 1966.[12] Some of the interpretations – such as those dealing with the need for negative security assurances (guarantees from nuclear-weapon states not to use or threaten to use nuclear weapons against those not possessing nuclear weapons) and the understanding that a non-proliferation treaty was a step towards nuclear disarmament rather than a goal in itself – remain at the root of shared and deeply held normative values among members of the Non-Aligned Movement.

Shaker observes that the unity among the eight non-aligned members of the ENDC was not the result of their association with any particular formal bloc or alliance (NAM itself was fairly young at the time), but was forged through the recognition and pursuit of common interests and goals. This unity, however, dissipated by the time the Soviet Union and the United States tabled identical drafts of the NPT in 1967. By then, some members of the group of eight had decided that divergent national interests required different responses to the Soviet and US draft text, leading to differences in their positions on and interpretations of particular items and language.[13] Ultimately, one of the eight non-aligned members of the ENDC (India) chose not to sign the NPT, another (Egypt) waited more than a decade before ratifying it, and a third (Brazil) waited for three decades.[14]

Non-aligned diversity at the inception of the NPT was a mixed blessing. On the one hand, it allowed individual states flexibility and space to bring their views and proposals to the table and gain the support of the group before presenting them to the larger bodies. NAM members thus obtained a greater presence at the nuclear negotiating table as a collective than they were likely to have achieved in their individual capacities. On the other hand, accommodating this diversity at times meant adopting a lowest common denominator position, or – such as at the final stages of the NPT negotiation – no common position at all.[15] Over time, and with the growth of the movement's membership and diversity, the tension between tolerating multiple voices and acting in concert has become more acute.

A defining moment for NAM on NPT matters occurred at the 1995 NPT Review and Extension Conference. During that month-long negotiation in New York, in accordance with Article VIII of the treaty, states parties were to decide if the NPT should continue in force indefinitely or be extended for a limited period. The countries of the global North (the West and former Socialist bloc) were united in their support for an indefinite extension. The Non-Aligned Movement, however, was conflicted and unable to forge a common position in advance of or during the conference.[16] A group of like-minded NAM states led by Indonesia, for example, argued for a 25-year rolling extension of the treaty linked to specific disarmament commitments, but even within that group, agreement could not be reached until late in the conference. Mexico initially proposed successive five-year extensions, also subject to achieving progress on disarmament goals, but did not actively seek to build support for its position. Venezuela reportedly advocated 'its own special version of a 25-year "rolled over" extension'.[17] While NAM was unable to reach agreement internally on its approach, support at the conference grew for the Canadian proposal, which endorsed indefinite extension without conditions related to progress in disarmament or further implementation of other aspects of the treaty.[18]

At the outset of the conference, it became clear that one of the newest NAM members – South Africa – would play a major role. The opening statement by the South African Foreign Minister Alfred Nzo was a conceptual *tour de force*, and was recognised by many observers as instrumental in enabling Conference President Jayantha Dhanapala to build a compromise package that included indefinite extension of the treaty.[19] Ironically, to ensure NAM support for the indefinite extension, South Africa first had to work against the 25-year rolling extension idea advanced by the movement's leading states.[20] Its success in this matter was a function of the moral clout enjoyed by the Mandela government and the prowess of South African diplomats, as well as a testament to the great value NAM states attached to the treaty. The essence of the South African proposal was a combination of initiatives, which included a strengthened treaty review process and a set of disarmament and non-proliferation principles, along with the decision to extend the treaty indefinitely. These three elements, slightly modified by Indonesia to include a reference to 'objectives' as well as 'principles', became the basis for the package of decisions that was eventually adopted by consensus.[21] The final element of the treaty-extension deal was the Resolution on the Middle East, co-sponsored by the three NPT depositaries – Russia, the United Kingdom and the United States – which called on all states in the region to join the NPT and take steps towards the establishment of a zone free of nuclear and other weapons of mass destruction in the Middle East. This fourth element proved necessary to meet the demands of the Arab group led by Egypt.

Just as NAM was indispensable for the successful extension of the 1995 Conference, it was also instrumental in making possible the adoption by consensus of the 2000 NPT Review Conference Final Document. This vigorously negotiated document exceeded the expectations of most participants and observers at the time and was especially notable for the adoption of an 'unequivocal undertaking by the nuclear-weapon states to accomplish the total elimination of their nuclear arsenals' and the so-called 13 Practical Steps 'for the systematic and progressive efforts' to achieve nuclear disarmament.[22]

NAM's impact on the 2000 NPT Rev Con Final Document was less the result of NAM's position as a cohesive political grouping and more the product of the active engagement by several of its members and observers in the New Agenda

Coalition (NAC), a cross-regional, cross-bloc group of seven states united in their objective to achieve greater progress on disarmament. This small but influential group consisted of Brazil, Egypt, Ireland, Mexico, New Zealand, South Africa and Sweden.[23] The origins of the coalition can be traced back to the 1995 Review and Extension Conference, at which Ireland, Sweden and Austria broke away from the European Union position on nuclear-disarmament issues.[24]

While NAM adopted quite a confrontational approach in the run-up to the 2000 Rev Con, the NAC successfully positioned itself as 'the only reasonable group with whom NWS [nuclear-weapons states] could engage'.[25] Led by a number of very talented diplomats, the NAC was able to provide a major bridge between the non-nuclear and nuclear-weapons states, and managed to negotiate much stronger language on disarmament in the Final Document than had been achieved at prior review conferences. Although all members of the NAC acted in their national capacities, the inclusion in the coalition of such leading non-aligned states as Egypt, South Africa, Mexico and Brazil gave the negotiated deal great standing with the movement as a whole, and NAM was prepared to accept it, both because of its content and the role NAM members had played in its negotiation.[26]

A decade of estrangement

While the first post-Cold War decade saw the strengthening of the NPT and the active involvement of non-aligned countries such as Egypt, Brazil, Mexico and South Africa in building bridges between the nuclear- and non-nuclear-weapon states, the decade following that was marked by a sharp decline in multilateralism and a deepening divide between NAM and the West, especially the United States. Under the George W. Bush administration, the United States reneged on past NPT commitments, sought unfettered flexibility with respect to its nuclear activities, promoted a policy of 'non-proliferation exceptionalism' in which rules and regulations were applied differently to selected countries depending on their relationships with the United States, and generally eschewed nuclear disarmament initiatives.[27] From the vantage point of NAM – and much of the rest of the world – the US focus was on preventing nuclear weapons from 'falling into the wrong hands' rather than eliminating the weapons themselves. During this period, Washington was not even inclined to pursue legally binding non-proliferation measures, investing instead in either unilateral action or that by 'coalitions of the willing'.

The Bush administration's decision to oppose the CTBT, which many states within and outside of NAM regard as a litmus test of commitment to the NPT, was especially objectionable to NAM. In place of negotiated treaties, Washington promoted unilateral and plurilateral non-proliferation measures such as the Proliferation Security Initiative. In addition, Washington's emphasis on legislating non-proliferation commitments for all UN members by means of Security Council-mandated resolutions was deeply unsettling to NAM (and also raised concerns on the part of some Western states such as Canada), which had long questioned the fairness and transparency of the UNSC dominated by the nuclear-weapons states.

A number of nuclear-proliferation developments during the first decade of the twenty-first century also contributed to the deterioration of the US/West–NAM relationship: the North Korean announcement of its withdrawal from the NPT; revelations of Iranian nuclear transgressions; and the uncovering of a vast, illicit nuclear-trafficking network linked to Pakistan's A.Q. Khan. Not only did these events involve a number of NAM countries, but the movement's reluctance to condemn the behaviour of its members in a timely and forceful fashion fuelled US suspicions about the nuclear motivations of certain NAM states and reinforced the demand for more stringent non-proliferation measures, including restrictions on sensitive nuclear technology.[28]

As indicated earlier, the end of the Cold War and the disintegration of the Soviet bloc confronted the Non-Aligned Movement with an existential crisis. On the one hand, from the standpoint of its core value structure, NAM could only welcome the demise of superpower rivalry and the potential to recast and refocus international dynamics on North–South issues involving economic and developmental concerns. On the other hand, the loss of its traditional protagonists, especially with regard to disarmament matters, required the movement to redefine itself in ways not dependent on opposition to the policies of the United States and the Soviet Union/ Russia.[29] Although difficult, this was not an impossible task, as non-alignment had never signified equidistance from Moscow and Washington. As Cedric Grant points out, non-alignment was not only based on opposition to the two superpowers, but on safeguarding the interests of NAM members without reference to great-power politics – interests which were first and foremost related to international socio-economic inequities.[30]

The election of President Barack Obama in 2008 and the accompanying reorientation of US policy towards support for multilateral institutions, international treaties and nuclear disarmament were viewed positively, though cautiously, by many non-aligned states. They were particularly welcoming of Obama's 2009 speech in Prague, which recommitted the United States to the goal of a world free of nuclear weapons. The speech raised hopes and expectations in many capitals that it would be possible to move forward on an ambitious programme to achieve deep reductions in nuclear weapons and to strengthen the NPT. This greatly improved, optimistic atmosphere was in evidence at the meeting of the 2009 NPT Preparatory Committee (Prep Com), which convened for two weeks in New York in May 2009. Many delegates appeared content to savour the absence of harsh US rhetoric on previously divisive issues and were prepared to give the new administration in Washington the benefit of the doubt. The bar for success at the Prep Com had been set so low that, when the chair was able to gain consensus on the agenda for the 2010 Review Conference at the outset of the meeting, many delegates were prepared to declare it a success without making a concerted effort to negotiate any substantive recommendations.[31] While China and France seemed particularly unprepared to negotiate further on substance, NAM itself was divided on how best to proceed. This was most apparent during the final days of the Prep Com, when NAM chose to support the chair's call to halt the review of draft recommendations in order to preserve the positive atmosphere. At this time, NAM delegates from Brazil, Chile and Nigeria joined with the United Kingdom in challenging the statement by Indonesia, which spoke on behalf of NAM, that it was time to congratulate the Prep Com chair on a job well done and conclude the meeting.[32] These NAM and NWS representatives asserted that sufficient time remained to attempt to forge consensus on a number of disarmament, non-proliferation and peaceful-use recommendations, based on earlier drafts circulated by the chair of the meeting.

Notwithstanding the generally positive atmosphere at and outcome of the 2009 Prep Com, NAM was not ready to conclude that a fundamental change had taken place in US nuclear-disarmament policy or that the other NWS were serious in matching the rhetoric of disarmament with concrete actions. In the words of one senior diplomat from a leading NAM state, 'trust is not built on words. We have heard this all before. When the NWS demonstrate their commitment by deeds, we will respond in kind.'[33] Many other NAM members had similar reservations, based on past disappointments, and were very much in a 'wait and see' mode, hopeful that a sea change would occur but not yet prepared to lower the levees.

Although the Obama administration believed that it was rapidly moving to implement a forward-looking disarmament and non-proliferation agenda, the long-standing distrust between the United States and NAM led the two parties to assess some of Obama's early initiatives in very different ways. Illustrative of this divergence was the dissonance produced by Washington's promotion of a new United Nations Security Council Resolution on Disarmament and Non-proliferation in September 2009 (adopted as UNSCR 1887). From the US perspective, this initiative – linked to a heads of state/government summit at the Security Council chaired by Obama – was indicative of the renewed US commitment to the United Nations and support for international instruments for pursuing nuclear disarmament and non-proliferation. From the perspective of NAM, the manner by which the resolution was adopted was heavy-handed, while its content was light on disarmament, heavy on non-proliferation and counter-nuclear terrorism, and virtually silent on the need to implement the 1995 NPT Review and Extension Conference Resolution on the Middle East.[34] As a consequence, leading NAM states were anxious to underline that the resolution should not serve as the basis for any kind of agreement in the NPT context. NAM also insisted on removing all references to UNSCR 1887 from draft resolutions at the UN General Assembly First Committee in autumn 2009.

The successful conclusion of the New START (Strategic Arms Reductions Treaty) by the United States and Russia in early 2010 and the release of a new US Nuclear Posture Review that reduced US reliance on nuclear weapons were received positively by many NAM members. The consensus Communiqué and Work Plan adopted by 47 heads of state/government at the April 2010 Nuclear Security Summit in Washington, to which a number of leading NAM members subscribed, also could be viewed as evidence that the United States (and other NWS) were making good on some of their prior pledges. These developments, however, occurred very close to the start of the 2010 Review Conference and provided little opportunity for the Non-Aligned Movement to adjust its positions in advance of the May conference.

NAM and the 2010 Review Conference
Negotiating behaviour

NAM came to the 2010 conference with an ambitious, forward-looking set of disarmament objectives and recommendations, including a call for setting a specific deadline for the complete elimination of nuclear weapons. A number of other non-nuclear-weapons states, particularly those in Western Europe, also supported the idea of a timeline and endorsed other planks in the NAM platform, including a nuclear-weapons convention that would prohibit the production, stockpiling and use of nuclear weapons, as well as provide for their elimination. The NAM working paper on disarmament, however, was notable for the early date it set for achievement of a nuclear-weapon-free world – 2025 – and the steps it outlined as necessary in order for this goal to be accomplished. The more general NAM working paper contained an impressive 81 recommendations covering the three pillars of the treaty.[35] Although it soon became clear that there was little common ground between the NAM papers and the nuclear-weapons states' positions, neither NAM nor the other political groupings at the Rev Con initially displayed much readiness to compromise.

This initial inflexibility was apparent in the collective NAM responses to the draft documents tabled by the chairs of the three main committees dealing with disarmament, non-proliferation and peaceful use and the three subsidiary bodies focused respectively on nuclear disarmament and security assurances, regional issues including implementation of the 1995 Middle East resolution, and 'other provisions of the treaty' (for example, those dealing with the withdrawal of members).[36] NAM presented numerous amendments to the draft documents that often were restatements of text from the NAM working papers. Rather than signalling a seriousness of purpose about specific NAM positions, this 'laundry list' style of response gave the appearance of inflexibility and unreasonableness, at least in the eyes of NAM's Western counterparts.[37]

This impression was reinforced by the overall tendency for deliberations on the conference floor to amount to verbatim readings of different parties' proposed amendments, without much interactive debate or discussion. The movement as a collective did not appear to have a 'fall back' position, nor did it – or other political groupings, including the EU – display a willingness to engage in bridge-building activities during the conference negotiations. Only in the last several days of the conference did the Non-Aligned chair, Egyptian Ambassador Maged Abdelaziz start to refer to certain positions as 'red lines', suggesting that other points in the draft final document were open to negotiation. This development appeared to come as a surprise to some of the non-NAM diplomats.[38]

What Western diplomats perceived as NAM intransigence was, to a large extent, a function of the movement's structure and modus operandi. NAM's relatively non-hierarchical decision-making process meant that any state could introduce amendments to be included in the group response, and unless other states expressly objected to an amendment it would become part of the group position.[39] At the same time, the large size of the group left very little time for deliberation of proposed changes, consideration of what might be acceptable to all sides or agreement upon a compromise position. Furthermore, as the movement tends to be non-confrontational in its internal deliberations, clashes of opinion are relatively rare and unwelcome, and it is not *comme il faut* to question another member's motivations and positions. Therefore, states that do not toe the general line are more likely to take an independent position in a national capacity than to try to change the movement's stance. Conversely, states that need the cover of a 'group stance' are more likely to expend greater effort and engage higher representation in internal policy discussions for the purpose of shaping the collective position. As a result, on certain issues the collective NAM voice is more ideological and extreme than that of many of its individual members.

On occasion, the reluctance to contest each other's positions – or simply the perseverance of some members – can produce NAM texts that contradict the movement's own long-standing principles and high-level negotiated positions. An example of this occurred on 18 May at the Rev Con, when NAM delivered its formal response to the draft report of the chair of the Main Committee II. One of the proposed edits from the negotiated NAM text was to strike the wording 'on the basis of arrangements freely arrived at among the States of the region concerned' from the reference to nuclear-weapon-free zones.[40] This amendment, introduced in the intra-NAM deliberations by Syria (as it also did at the UN First Committee in 2009), was directly at odds with a host of previously negotiated documents of great importance to NAM, including the 1978 Final Document of the First UNGA Special Session on Disarmament, not to mention the final declarations of the NAM Summits of Heads of States and Government.[41] Nonetheless, it showed up in the collective NAM response to the chair's drafts on at least two occasions. Even though most non-aligned states are parties to nuclear-weapon-free zone agreements, it appears that the majority of delegates involved in internal NAM deliberations at that stage either were not sufficiently familiar with this issue or did not deem it worth their while to contest the contradictory language with Syria. Experienced diplomats from Brazil, Chile and Nigeria had to speak against the NAM amendment in their national capacity on the conference floor. Later, these countries were able to prevent the amendment from being again adopted as part of the NAM feedback – this time, to the draft Final Document, leaving Syria to speak in its national capacity on the conference floor to advance its contrary position.

Key NAM players

At the opening of the conference, Indonesian Foreign Minister Marty Natalegawa provided the Rev Con with a boost of positive energy by announcing that his country was beginning the process of ratifying the CTBT. Subsequently, however, Egypt took centre stage and played the most prominent role among NAM states at the conference. As NAM chair, Egypt proved to be a masterful and shrewd leader at the Rev Con, in part by very accurately gauging the sentiments of the movement's members and recognising the parameters within which it could operate. Although Egyptian policy obviously was the product of a bureaucratic decision-making process, it also reflected the personality and perspective of the Permanent Representative in New York, Maged Abdelaziz. As the head of a very large delegation, he was able to call upon a number of other experienced diplomats to coordinate the different roles that Egypt played at the Review Conference – NAM chair, NAC chair and national delegate. Egypt also took the initiative in coordinating NAM positions and responses to draft conference documents, a role that in New York was usually performed by the Coordinator of the Disarmament Working Group rather than the NAM chair.

Iran, designated by the West as the most likely spoiler in advance of the conference, presented a dual persona, with the less visible one being more flexible than expected. In the relatively open sessions of main committees and plenaries, Iran often employed delaying tactics of a procedural nature, and in closed-door consultations it also demonstrated a mastery of 'negotiation by attrition', prolonging the deliberations and wearing down its counterparts with a steady stream of interventions. It used the latter technique to good effect during the last week of the conference, for example, when the president instructed interested parties to negotiate particularly contentious paragraphs on safeguards. In the intense behind-the-scenes negotiations on the Middle East, however, Iran appeared to recognise the leadership role of Egypt and, reportedly, took a relatively constructive stance.[42] Overall, it was careful not to be identified as the party responsible for blocking consensus and sinking the conference. When on the last day of the Rev Con it became clear that the United States was ready to accept the final document explicitly calling on Israel to accede to the NPT and to place its nuclear facilities under comprehensive IAEA safeguards, Iranian representatives urgently sought instructions from Tehran to enable them to support the consensus.

Since 1980, the president of the Rev Con has been a representative from a NAM member or observer state.[43] Although this affiliation has not always ensured a successful outcome, it has frequently proved crucial in fashioning a consensus decision. The 2010 Rev Con was no exception, and President Libran Cabactulan from the Philippines made effective use of his fellow NAM diplomats, both formally and informally, during the month-long negotiation. He also had unusually visible support from the highest levels of his national government, which organised a large meeting of key diplomats and outside experts in Manila in February 2010 to assist him in preparing for the Review Conference. In addition to the support provided by his own delegation, Cabactulan relied heavily on a very small group of informal advisers, who were not directly associated with NAM. He also was adept at delegating authority to other experienced diplomats both within and outside of NAM.

Some typically vocal NAM members assumed a lower profile during the 2010 Rev Con than in the past. One such case was South Africa, a NAM (and New Agenda Coalition) member with particular moral clout on issues of nuclear disarmament and non-proliferation, and one that played a crucial role in forging agreements at the 1995 and 2000 conferences that were acceptable to both NAM and the NWS. At the 2010 Review Conference, interventions by the South African delegation were less numerous and consequential – at least on the conference floor. South Africa did not appear to play a leadership role in bridging intra-NAM positions or putting new proposals and initiatives on the table. In part, this less active approach can be explained by a preference for engaging in smaller group meetings. In addition, South Africa may have been wary of assuming a conspicuous bridge-building role, having witnessed the backtracking by the NWS on deals that it had helped to broker in 1995 and 2000. That said, some of the experienced South African diplomats engaged actively behind the scenes – most importantly, in the small Focus Group convened by the president to narrow differences on the most contentious issues before the conference.[44]

Disarmament at the 2010 Rev Con: do you know what's worth fighting for?

Before the Review Conference started, it was widely anticipated that progress on nuclear disarmament would be one of the factors required for a successful outcome. It was far from clear, however, how much progress was necessary or what specific language would be needed to secure a consensus final document. In this regard, the NAM working paper on nuclear disarmament was not of much help in gauging the movement's expectations and fault lines. As previously mentioned, NAM submitted two common working papers to the 2010 Rev Con, one of which focused exclusively on disarmament. Rather than separately addressing such issues as nuclear testing, a fissile material ban, negative security assurances, and so on, the movement took its cue from the 2009 Prep Com chair's draft paper and tabled a proposal on a comprehensive nuclear-disarmament action plan. The proposed plan was divided into five-year periods and set 2025 as the deadline for complete elimination of nuclear weapons.[45] A time-bound framework for nuclear disarmament had been part of the NAM position for decades, but a specific date was a new feature. The choice of 2025 as the deadline appears to have been influenced by the report of the International Commission on Nuclear Non-proliferation and Disarmament, co-chaired by Australia and Japan. The Comprehensive Action Agenda proposed by the commission indicated 2025 as a medium-term deadline for achievement of a 'minimization point' characterised by low numbers of nuclear warheads, adoption of no-first-use doctrines, entry into force of the fissile-material treaty and other measures. Many in NAM found this objective too modest, but the date was adopted for the more ambitious proposal for complete nuclear disarmament.[46]

The combination of steps proposed for the first phase of the action plan (2010–15) also contributed to confusion about NAM's goals and expectations. It contained both modest and highly ambitious objectives and was at times oddly repetitive or illogical, as some of the proposed steps seemed to compete with each other. For example, under the 'measures aimed at reducing the nuclear threat', the plan envisioned *concurrent* negotiations and early conclusion of agreements on a treaty banning the production of fissile material for nuclear weapons; unconditional and legally binding negative-security assurances; prohibition of the use or threat of use of nuclear weapons; 'a phased programme for the complete elimination of nuclear weapons', including a nuclear-weapons convention; and, among other things, establishment of an NWFZ in the Middle East. For the same five-year period, 'measures aimed at nuclear disarmament' contained, among others, full implementation of the nuclear weapons-states' 'disarmament obligations and commitments' under the NPT, including the 13 Practical Steps; further nuclear arms reductions (also referred to as START); placement of the fissile material removed from military use under IAEA safeguards, and the declaration of a nuclear disarmament decade (2010–20).

One of the reasons for the maximalist stance taken in the NAM disarmament working paper is that it was meant to represent the group's long-standing aspirations regarding nuclear disarmament, rather than actual expectations of the conference outcome. The inclusion of seemingly competing or conflicting proposed measures within the same timeframe might also have been the result of NAM's traditional resistance to a step-by-step approach in which the conclusion of one treaty (for example, the Fissile Material Cut-off Treaty) is viewed as a prerequisite for progressing to other measures. The formulation of the proposed action plan, however, muddled the message and contributed to the confusion among many diplomats outside of NAM. Staking out a maximalist position, according to some NAM diplomats, was also a deliberate strategy to offset the NWS argument that enough progress on disarmament had been achieved in recent years and it was now the turn of the non-nuclear-weapon states to make concessions on non-proliferation. Furthermore, the articulation of extreme positions can be viewed as a means to create space for the moderates to manoeuvre and negotiate progressive and pragmatic outcomes. However, although this strategy worked in the run-up to the 2000 Rev Con, it was less effective in 2010. Rather than setting the bar for the conference outcome high, the NAM paper appeared to many delegations to be as confusing as it was ambitious. It also did not signal a serious negotiating position.[47] Indeed, the most striking impression one receives from examining the NAM disarmament action plan is that of a lack of focus. A convention banning nuclear weapons (NWC), which could have served as the central feature of the movement's demand for a multilateral negotiated disarmament framework, received only a parenthetical mention in the working paper. Comparing the Final Document and the disarmament action plan contained therein with the NAM paper reveals a tremendous gap between the movement's stated position and the outcome of the conference.

A somewhat clearer indication of the goals and expectations of selected NAM states should be derived from the actual statements made by delegations at the Rev Con. Interestingly, relatively few NAM states referred to the proposed deadline that was part of the collective NAM paper, but rather limited their call to a time-bound framework without a specific date. Their statements explicitly endorsed the negotiation of a nuclear-weapons convention.[48] For example, the opening remarks by Indonesian Foreign Minister Natalegawa on behalf of NAM states party to the NPT noted that:

> The consideration of a Nuclear Weapons Convention
> banning all nuclear weapons, as mentioned in Article
> VI of the Treaty, should begin and should be an inte-

gral part of any plan of action on nuclear disarmament
to be adopted by this Conference.[49]

Significantly, several European states – Austria, Norway and
Switzerland – also spoke in support of a time-bound framework, and several more non-NAM countries endorsed the
idea of a nuclear-weapons convention (NWC). Although this
concept enjoyed considerable support at the Rev Con, the
final consensus text on Conclusions and Recommendations
referenced it only in the context of noting the five-point
nuclear-disarmament proposal by the UN Secretary-General.[50]
Evidently, neither NAM nor other states were prepared to make
the issue a make-or-break item for the Review Conference,
although the proposal held out the promise of bridging the
NAM and non-NAM nuclear-disarmament divide in the future.

During the general debate and the beginning of the work
of Main Committee I (on disarmament), many delegations,
including those from non-NAM states, argued that the final
document should build on the agreements achieved in 2000,
and that simply repeating the 13 Practical Steps was not enough.
Brazil, South Africa, Norway, Egypt, Algeria, Switzerland,
Nigeria, Venezuela and Indonesia were among those making
this case.[51] In the end, however, much of the action involved
a damage-limitation approach in which pitched battles were
waged to keep the 2010 outcome from regressing in comparison to the disarmament language adopted in 2000. Although
this was not a desirable outcome for many in NAM, it was not
sufficient to lead them to oppose the Final Document.

One new issue that enlivened the disarmament debate at the
2010 Rev Con focused on consideration of nuclear weapons in
the context of international humanitarian law. This initiative
was led not by NAM but by Switzerland, which, with support
from Austria, described nuclear weapons as 'immoral and

illegal'. Switzerland argued that there were no circumstances under which the use of nuclear weapons would be justifiable or permissible under international humanitarian law.[52] Although this was not their own idea, the initiative gained wide support among NAM delegations, and Latin American states in particular endorsed the application of international humanitarian law in assessing the legitimacy of nuclear weapons. The fact that it proved possible to include consensus language in the Final Document that expressed 'concern at the catastrophic humanitarian consequences of any use of nuclear weapons'[53] suggests that, in the future, the applicability of international humanitarian law may be another cross-cutting disarmament issue that can transcend political groupings and regions.

Overall, for what was supposed to be a make-or-break issue, NAM settled for a final document with a fairly modest disarmament section. This result is especially notable considering that the movement's headline ideas – a time-bound framework and a convention banning nuclear weapons – received significant support from non-NAM states and were viewed sympathetically by the chair of Subsidiary Body 1, Austrian Ambassador Alexander Marschik, who initially tabled an ambitious draft action plan. NAM's ultimate readiness to accept a much more modest disarmament package was the result of a combination of factors, including broad recognition that the conference needed an outcome; the priority attached by the NAM chair to an agreement on the Middle East; and of the focus on beating back proposals to strengthen verification and endorse multilateral fuel-cycle approaches. An underlying factor that also helps explain NAM acquiescence is the current, stagnant state of disarmament debate within NAM. In principle, nuclear disarmament remains the overall goal in context of the NPT, but there is a lack of powerful advocates today within the movement who 'own' the issue. India, once a powerful voice for disarmament (albeit from outside the NPT), lost its credibility after the 1998 nuclear tests and lately has been playing an unhelpful role on disarmament matters within the movement.[54] The NAM-affiliated members of the New Agenda Coalition (Brazil, Egypt, Mexico and South Africa), while still speaking strongly in support of nuclear disarmament, have focused increasingly on other priorities, though this trend might change in the new review cycle. Also absent is a more specific objective that serves to focus the states' energy and effort as there has been in the past – for example, when Mexico was able to mobilise the movement in support of the CTBT even at the risk of a failed Rev Con. That was precisely what transpired in 1990 when NAM chose to bring down the Review Conference rather than accept an outcome document without a commitment to the CTBT. The movement also succeeded, with the assistance of some of the Western European disarmament advocates, in making conclusion of the CTBT by 1996 a requirement for the indefinite extension of the NPT in 1995.

Today, not even the nuclear-weapons convention appears to command such commitment among NAM members in the context of the NPT.[55] Similarly, although most NAM members support some version of a Fissile Material Cut-off Treaty (FMCT) – often referred to as the next logical step for disarmament[56] – many are inclined to see it mainly as a Western priority. NAM, except for India, also argues that a treaty banning only future production is a mere non-proliferation, rather than a disarmament, measure and (along with several Western countries) insists that the issue of existing stocks be addressed in the negotiations of any fissile-material treaty. However, since the negotiations have not started, the question of existing stocks under an FMCT is not yet a mobilising issue.[57]

One of the effects of the decade of estrangement has been the increased fixation and energy spent by NAM states on resisting new non-proliferation measures and (perceived) restrictions on peaceful uses. Nuclear disarmament might seem a lofty but ephemeral goal at a time when infringements on the right to peaceful uses and nuclear cooperation are perceived as real and immediate. At least until very recently, this view was reinforced by the deep and widespread disenchantment within NAM about the seriousness of NWS toward the disarmament commitments they undertook in 1995 and 2000. This lack of faith in the ability to move the disarmament agenda forward made pursuit of a maximalist approach more attractive, and in some instances almost a default position. It remains to be seen if the change in US orientation and the growth in support from Western European states for disarmament initiatives such as a time-bound framework, which previously were dubbed 'distractions', will lead to an internal reassessment by NAM of its own positions and priorities, and whether it will facilitate engagement across ideological or geographical groupings. The period leading up to the 2015 NPT Review Conference will show if a new group of disarmament champions – from within and/or outside NAM – emerges to effectively move into the space that appeared vacant at the 2010 Rev Con.[58]

The interesting case of the Additional Protocol

As emphasised previously, NAM is far from homogenous, but the relationship between individual countries and the movement's 'official' positions is often misunderstood. Individual expressions of opinion can be perceived (or deliberately presented) as representing the non-aligned position overall, and conversely, the 'official' NAM positions might be taken as reflecting the views of all its members. In practice, NAM views on a particular issue can be quite diverse, and nowhere was this phenomenon more visible at the Rev Con than with respect to debate over proposals to universalise the IAEA Additional Protocol (AP).

The Additional Protocol, as the name suggests, is designed to supplement a state's standard safeguards agreement with the IAEA. A Model AP was negotiated at the IAEA in the 1990s, largely in response to the revelations of Iraq's nuclear-weapons programme and the agency's inability to detect it through the implementation of existing safeguards measures. The AP provides the IAEA with additional tools and access to not only verify the non-diversion of declared nuclear material, but also to detect undeclared nuclear material and activities in a state.[59]

There is an impression among the Western political grouping of states that NAM opposes the Additional Protocol in principle. A Japanese delegate voiced this point of view on the conference floor when he lamented that it was 'sad and depressing' that over 100 NAM states parties to the NPT disliked the Additional Protocol. In reality, no consensus view of the AP exists in the movement; many NAM states have the Additional Protocol in force, and there is a broad recognition that it as a valuable non-proliferation instrument. Disagreement centres on whether universalisation of the AP is a priority and whether the protocol should be obligatory for non-nuclear-weapons states as part of the verification standard under the NPT.

Among the more than 70 NAM members that have signed the AP, some believe the protocol should be universal, but only through the process of voluntary acceptance, while others support the Western preference for making it obligatory. States in the latter category are primarily those with relatively close relationships with the United States (such as Singapore) and countries that aim to benefit from nuclear cooperation with the United States in the immediate future, such as the United Arab Emirates. These countries were among the very few within the ranks of NAM to openly voice their support for the AP as a verification *standard*. However, an examination of national statements by NAM members in Main Committee II dealing with non-proliferation matters reveals that a wide variety of non-aligned states, from Indonesia to Mongolia to South Africa, spoke of the importance of broader acceptance of the Additional Protocol.

Why, then, is there tendency by outsiders to misunderstand the movement's position on the issue and to assume that most NAM members are opposed to the AP? In part, this stems from the language of the NAM working papers themselves. The working paper submitted by the movement to the 2010 Rev Con, while making no direct mention of the Additional Protocol, manages to convey principled opposition to recognition of the AP as the verification standard. The relevant recommendation reads:

> it is fundamental to make a distinction between legal obligations and voluntary confidence-building measures, in order to ensure that such voluntary undertakings are not turned into legal safeguard obligations.[60]

Thus, even though there is no internal NAM consensus regarding universalisation of the AP, the opposite impression is conveyed by language in the formal NAM working paper. Furthermore, while many NAM states may accept the Additional Protocol, they are reluctant to engage in an intra-NAM confrontation over the matter. As a result, in deliberations on the conference floor and in closed-door negotiations, the most active and assertive NAM voices that address the AP are those that most oppose it. They also tend to belong to some of the most influential actors in the movement, who are prepared to invest great energy and effort to shape the joint NAM language on the matter.

The most vocal opponents of the Additional Protocol as the verification standard are Brazil and states from the Middle East.[61] Brazil, as a NAM observer, makes the case on principled grounds, arguing for a more equitable balance between disarmament and non-proliferation measures. It also cautions that linking AP implementation to compliance under Article III of the NPT, which deals with IAEA safeguards, would amount to a re-interpretation of the treaty. As one Brazilian delegate to the Rev Con put it: 'We come to New York as a country in compliance and will not leave as a country in noncompliance.' In addition to this principled objection, Brazil – along with former NAM member Argentina – has a more idiosyncratic concern about the Additional Protocol due to its special safeguards arrangement with the IAEA through the Quadripartite Agreement.[62] Brazil is intent on protecting its centrifuge enrichment programme from additional verification burdens.[63] At the IAEA, Brazil and Argentina tend to work in tandem in their national capacities to reject any initiative that suggests that the AP is obligatory, while in the NPT context Brazil couches its opposition in terms of NAM principles and employs the movement as a foreign-policy tool to promote its national position.[64]

Iran's stance on the Additional Protocol – that adherence must be of a voluntary nature – is conditioned by its own nuclear programme and by the Security Council's demand that Tehran fully implement the protocol. Egypt maintains a similar posture, but for a different reason. Its position has little to do with the substance of the Additional Protocol and everything to do with its broader refusal to undertake additional non-proliferation commitments before Israel accedes to the NPT. At a minimum, it insists that there must first be meaningful progress in establishing a zone free of nuclear weapons (and other weapons of mass destruction) in the Middle East. Most other Arab states follow Egypt's lead on this linkage, although as noted above, some states, such as the United Arab Emirates, may deviate from the common position if national energy and trade interests so dictate.

It is important to note that the Additional Protocol has not always been a particularly controversial and divisive issue for NAM. The Non-Aligned Movement was initially broadly supportive of the AP, which was negotiated in the aftermath of revelations about Iraq's nuclear programme, although it did not regard universalisation of the AP as a priority. For example, at the 2000 NPT Review Conference many non-aligned delegations, including Egypt, welcomed the negotiation of the Model Additional Protocol as a measure that strengthened the safeguards regime.[65] Some NAM countries, particularly those in Southeast Asia, even suggested that universal acceptance of the Additional Protocol could help eliminate 'undue' export-control restrictions – a stance that in retrospect could be interpreted as endorsement of the AP as a condition of supply. A leading NAM state, South Africa, submitted a working paper on safeguards to the 2000 Rev Con, which contained language proposing that 'all States Parties should also sign and bring into force the Additional Protocol to Safeguards Agreements'.[66]

This early support of the AP, however, waned in some countries as the decade of estrangement wore on and US rejection of the commitments of 1995 and 2000 concerning disarmament and the Middle East was accompanied by increasing pressure for new non-proliferation measures and a focus on preventing nuclear terrorism. The Western push to universalise the Additional Protocol as an obligatory measure also came against the backdrop of growing US unilateralism, the invasion of Iraq (in spite of the conclusions of the UN's Monitoring, Verification and Inspection Commission), lack of progress on disarmament and a generally dismissive attitude towards the concerns of developing non-nuclear countries. The United

States, for example, stated in its 2004 Prep Com working paper: 'implementation of the Protocol should become a key standard by which to measure an NPT party's commitment ... The Protocol,' it maintained, 'should become a condition of nuclear supply by the end of 2005.'[67] At the same meeting, commenting on the chair's summary, the US delegate emphasised that the United States did not 'support all 13 practical steps' or 'a mechanism to promote implementation of the 1995 resolution on the Middle East'.[68] The United States further questioned the relevance of negative security assurances – a long-standing NAM demand – and suggested that nuclear threats from NPT violators and non-state actors were more serious. The debate over the AP was thus transformed into a debate about principles and the balance of NPT rights and obligations, a development that Iran used to influence the collective NAM stance on the Additional Protocol.

This change in NAM's thinking about the AP is also reflected in the working papers submitted by the movement at Prep Com meetings after the 2000 Review Conference. NAM working papers submitted to the Preparatory Committee meetings in 2002, 2003 and 2004 all contained language stressing 'the importance of the IAEA's Safeguards system, including comprehensive safeguards agreements and also the Model Additional Protocols'.[69] At the same time, they cautioned that 'the Movement does not desire to see international efforts towards achieving universality of comprehensive safeguards to wither away in favour of pursuing additional measures and restrictions on non-nuclear-weapons states'.[70] The working paper tabled at the 2005 Review Conference for the first time stated: 'The Group emphasises that it is fundamental to make the distinction between legal obligations and voluntary confidence-building measures.'[71] This language became standard NAM parlance, despite the fact that more NAM states were adopting the Additional Protocol and many within NAM began to have second thoughts about how to deal with the Iranian nuclear issue. By 2010, even the sentence stressing the importance of IAEA safeguards and the Additional Protocol had disappeared from the NAM working paper.[72]

The shadow of NPT outliers at the Rev Con: the special case of India

One of the surreal qualities of NPT Review Conference delib-erations is the manner in which NPT member states often manage to avoid debate on many of the most pressing prolif-eration challenges. Issues that one might expect to be front and centre of debate – for example, the nuclear weapons tests by North Korea, the nuclear-arms race in South Asia and the risks posed by illicit nuclear-trafficking networks – more often than not are but minor blips on the NPT Review Conference radar, perhaps generating several national statements in the general debate, but rarely sustaining extended discussion. This tendency to pass on some of the most controversial issues extends to matters associated with Iran's nuclear activities and Syria's destroyed nuclear facility, which are much more likely to receive scrutiny at the IAEA in Vienna than at the NPT Rev Con in New York. Although NAM members are by no means the principal parties responsible for setting the Rev Con agenda or delimiting its focus, NAM often concurs with decisions that have the effect of removing some of the most contentious issues from active consideration in the review process.

One might have expected that the US–India nuclear deal and the corresponding decision by the Nuclear Suppliers Group (NSG) to exempt India from its guidelines would have followed the aforementioned pattern of neglect, especially as these initiatives were strongly supported by an unusual coali-tion of nuclear-weapon states and non-nuclear-weapons states.

In fact, however, the issue of nuclear trade with India was a point of major contention in all of the main committees of the 2010 NPT Review Conference and also revealed a major and lingering divide within the movement.

On the one hand, NAM as a collective was slow to appreciate the full import of the July 2005 announcement by the Bush administration that it planned to seek an entirely new approach to nuclear relations with India. Although NAM did not revise its prior position on the prohibition of nuclear trade with non-NPT parties – a stance adopted mainly with Israel in mind – it was initially remarkably silent about the implications of the proposed deal. Most members appear not to have thought through how the US policy shift and proposed NSG exemption for India might compromise the integrity of the NPT by appearing to reward non-NPT parties and nuclear-weapons possessors, while also diverting international attention from efforts to penalise Israel for its non-adherence to the treaty. On the other hand, once a number of Arab states – along with Iran – recognised how the India initiatives might compromise NAM's long-standing efforts to constrain Israel's nuclear programme, a number of NAM members sought to toughen the movement's position. Leading this effort were states in the Middle East, including Iran and its Arab neighbours. They were also joined by members from other regions who, in addition to a concern about obscuring policy directed at Israel, were disturbed by the obvious double standard between NAM's principled policy on disarmament and the benefits the proposed nuclear deal would bestow on a non-NPT state that had repeatedly tested nuclear weapons.

As Sverre Lodgaard points out, initially NAM was content to make use of the same formulation at the first Prep Com in 2007, following the announced change in US policy, as it did at the spring 2005 NPT Review Conference prior to the announcement of the deal.[73] In its working paper for the Prep Com, NAM called for

> total and complete prohibition of the transfer of all nuclear-related equipment, information, material and facilities, resources and devices, and the extension of assistance in the nuclear scientific or technological fields to States non-parties to the treaty without exception.[74]

This language, while tough, was a significantly watered-down version of text that had enjoyed widespread support within NAM but was opposed by several NPT countries speaking on India's behalf. The resulting compromise was reiteration in 2007 of a formula that had gained consensus prior to the announcement of the US–India deal, when the NAM position had been directed mainly at Israel.

Only in spring 2008, at the second NPT Prep Com, did NAM express more specific opposition to the nuclear cooperation agreement with India. At that time Indonesia, on behalf of NAM, indicated that:

> recent developments, in particular the nuclear cooperation agreement signed by a NWS with a non-party to the NPT is a matter of great concern, since in accordance with that agreement nuclear materials can be transferred to un-safeguarded facilities in violation of Article III, paragraph 2 of the NPT.[75]

This language was repeated at the 2009 NPT Prep Com, and again, verbatim, at the 2010 Review Conference, in the latter instance on the first day of the Rev Con in remarks by Indonesian Foreign Minister Marty Natalegawa, speaking on behalf of NAM.[76]

This apparent consensus formulation, however, concealed unusually heated and sustained debates within NAM over how far to criticise one of its own, a divergence of views that surfaced in a variety of intra-NAM meetings and at the IAEA Board of Governors, meetings of the Nuclear Suppliers Group, trilateral meetings involving Brazil, South Africa and India, and in the NPT Review Process. Particularly revealing, at times, was what was not said. Noticeable for its absence, for example, was any reference in the NAM Ministerial Statement in Tehran in late July 2008 to the US–India deal, notwithstanding the statement NAM had made on the subject at the 2008 NPT Prep Com that concluded only a few months earlier. NAM as a group was silent in Vienna in August 2008 on the India-specific safeguards agreement. It may not be coincidental that Iran was able to garner support at the meeting in Tehran for language very sympathetic toward its positions on domestic nuclear matters, while bowing to the preference of one founding NAM member who was not present at the Prep Com with respect to the omission of commentary on the issue of nuclear trade with non-NPT parties.[77] Unfortunately, one can only speculate about the content of the bilateral discussions between the Indian and Iranian foreign ministers during the Tehran meeting.

Also indicative of the debate within the movement over the India deal was NAM's decision not to put forward a collective statement before the August 2008 IAEA Board of Governors meeting, which addressed the issue of an India-specific safeguards agreement. Instead, NAM members on the board made interventions in their national capacity. Of the 15 NAM members that took the floor, all but four – Iraq, Egypt, Malaysia and Iran – supported the conclusion of the Indian-specific safeguards agreement with the IAEA, despite the deviation of the accord from the standard safeguards model.[78] An unusual situation thus emerged in which the majority of the nuclear have-nots on the board chose to align themselves with the United States and the other nuclear haves, at the same time that NAM was staking out a very different collective position in the context of the NPT review process.[79]

Unlike the IAEA Board, at the 2010 Rev Con, most of the NAM interventions on the subject of the US–India deal and the NSG exemption were very critical of the special treatment afforded India and the US position on this matter in particular. This criticism, led most aggressively by Arab NAM members and also Iran, surfaced in debates over disarmament, non-proliferation, regional security and peaceful use. It was perhaps most heated in Main Committee II (and Subsidiary Body 3) with respect to the issue of universality. Many states, including those from NAM, pointed out that the US–India deal and the related NSG exemption contradicted the 1995 NPT Review and Extension Conference Decision on Principles and Objectives for Nuclear Non-Proliferation and Disarmament, which required acceptance of full-scope safeguards as a precondition for all new nuclear-supply arrangements. Accordingly, in 2010 NAM sought to introduce language in the revised draft report by the chair of Main Committee II that not only new but also *existing* supply arrangements should be in accordance with this provision. This effort, pursued with particular vigour by several Arab states, appeared aimed at precluding the possibility that deals similar to the one concluded between the United States and India would be struck with Israel and Pakistan. Although most NSG members were unwilling to directly defend the exemption decision (which had been blessed by several key NAM members and observers, most notably South Africa and Brazil), the United States made it clear that it would not revisit the deal with New Delhi. In arguing against the inclusion of the term 'existing', the lead US spokesperson on issues before Main Committee II indicated that while the United States was prepared to reaffirm its commitment to the 1995 Principles and Objectives, it was in fact a political and not legal obligation, and that regardless of what the Rev Con chose to say on the matter, the United States would not revise its stance on the US–India deal.

This position, also supported by France, was viewed by many NAM states and others as suggesting that states could pick and choose which elements of NPT Rev Con decisions they care to implement while disavowing others that no longer took their fancy – an approach that made it very difficult to hold states to their NPT obligations, regardless of whether they were of a legally binding or political nature. In vague compromise language, the final conference document urged supplier states to ensure that exports did not 'directly or indirectly assist the development of nuclear weapons' and were 'in full conformity with the 1995 decision on Principles and Objectives on Nuclear Non-Proliferation and Disarmament'. Though it was perhaps necessary to bridge the gulf that existed at the time between the supporters and critics of the India deal, this compromise also exposed significant divisions within NAM, leading some to accuse Brazil and South Africa of adopting the same non-proliferation cherry-picking practices of which the NWS were so often guilty.[80] As one senior diplomat from the non-aligned camp acknowledged, when pressed to explain the apparent double standard: 'we have principles, and if you don't like them, we have other principles'.

2010: too close for comfort, or 'failure was not an option'?

For observers not privy to behind-the-scenes negotiations, the 2010 conference appeared to be headed for failure as it entered the last week. In often freezing, makeshift conference rooms in a temporary building next to the United Nations, parties endlessly restated their well-known positions. Not much more progress towards consensus could be gleaned from the protracted, informal consultations that were convened at the request of the Rev Con president behind closed doors during the last week on issues such as safeguards, the disarmament action plan and institutional reform. Yet, on the last day of the conference, following the cancellation of two scheduled plenary meetings, a Final Document with over five dozen concrete action items and recommendations was adopted by consensus. Conspicuous by their absence from the list of 64 items were many of NAM's prior disarmament demands, including a call for complete nuclear disarmament by 2025 and provision of legally binding negative-security assurances. Low-key grumbling among some NAM delegations about the outcome raised the question of how it came to pass.

Divisions among states parties on issues of disarmament, safeguards and peaceful uses ran as deep as ever.[81] In the absence of any evident bridge-builders, it became necessary for the President of the Conference Philippine Ambassador Libran Cabactulan to assemble a Focus Group of at least 16 states to meet separately in an effort to narrow differences on issues also under consideration by the three main committees.[82] This body's ability to strike a deal in tandem with the conclusion of parallel small-group negotiations on the Middle East on the penultimate day of the Rev Con made it possible for Cabactulan to announce the late breakthrough. Also contributing to the overall final agreement was the innovative composition of the Final Document, which consisted of a non-consensus review portion based on the president's reflections on what had transpired, as well as a forward-looking consensus-based action plan.[83]

The process by which decisions were reached at the Review Conference very much resembled a Russian *Matryoshka* doll with multiple layers, most of which were only vaguely visible to the majority of diplomats attending. Very close to, if not in, the innermost layer was the Focus Group, which had no formal conference membership or conference mandate but functioned at the bequest of Cabactulan, who asked the head of the Norwegian delegation, Steffen Kongstad, to facilitate its operation. The size of this group fluctuated between 16 and 24 members depending on the specific issues under consideration, but it usually included the five NWS (China, France, Russia, The UK and the US), Brazil, Cuba, Egypt, Germany, Iran, Indonesia, Japan, Mexico, Norway, Spain (which held the EU presidency at the time) and South Africa.[84] A number of NAM states – as well as many other delegations among the 172 represented at the Rev Con – appear not to have been aware of the existence of this small group or its crucial role in trying to find common ground on many of the most contentious issues before the Rev Con. Most of the key NAM members and observers, however, participated in the work of the Focus Group, including both moderate and more radical voices. This mixture was crucial in gaining acceptance of the Final Document.

There are differing accounts of how much representatives from the Focus Group briefed other members of their political groupings on the progress of negotiations. All of the NAM delegations in the Focus Group participated in their national capacity, but were of course cognisant of the movement's interests and expectations.[85] Due to the inclusion of some significant NAM players, most members of the movement apparently felt 'sufficiently represented' and had confidence that their interests were being protected.[86] Moreover, as leading NAM actors such as Egypt, South Africa, Mexico, Indonesia, Cuba and Iran were all represented in the group, no other NAM state was willing or able to press for additional concessions. Thus, notwithstanding their vocal, ideological positions and lack of enthusiasm for the content of the Final Document, states such as Venezuela, Libya and Syria were unable and unwilling to sway the movement or stand in the way of consensus. As a result, although the Final Document bore little resemblance to the NAM working paper on disarmament, it proved to be an acceptable bargain, securing modest gains on the disarmament front, conceding little in the way of new non-proliferation obligations and, most importantly, containing tentative steps forward in addressing the crucial issue of the Middle East.

It is unlikely that the deal negotiated by the Focus Group would have saved the conference without an agreement on steps towards implementation of the Middle East Resolution adopted at the 1995 NPT Review and Extension Conference. The issue was decisive for NAM chair Egypt and for the Arab Group in general. The rest of the movement recognised the importance of the issue to these representatives from the Middle East and essentially deferred to Egypt, despite the misgivings some had about other portions of the document. Intense negotiations between Egypt, the United States, Russia, the League of Arab States, Iran and the chair of Subsidiary Body 2 – Ambassador Alison Kelly from Ireland – produced an agreement to convene a Middle East conference in 2012 to address the establishment of a WMD-free zone in the region, and to appoint a facilitator to lead the preparations for the conference and assist in the implementation of the 1995 resolution.[87] The acceptance of this deal by all the relevant parties by noon of May 28 ensured that the Rev Con gained a consensus outcome.

Conclusions

The 2010 NPT Review Conference was, in many respects, a microcosm of NAM's nuclear politics, both internally and with respect to the broader international community. As such, it reveals a number of important features about NAM perspectives on nuclear issues and the relative influence on NAM policy of principled positions and pragmatic considerations.

What is perhaps most apparent from NAM's actions during the NPT review process in general, and the 2010 NPT Review Conference in particular, is the diversity of views within the Movement about nuclear priorities, the style by which collective positions are formulated, and the on-going tension within NAM between strict adherence to long-standing disarmament principles and goals and support for less than optimal positions that are necessary in order to reach consensus with the nuclear-weapons states.

As previously noted, internal NAM negotiations in the context of the NPT review process tend to be cumbersome due to the sheer size of the movement, the diversity of views held by its membership, and the non-hierarchical style of decision-making in large intra-NAM meetings during which most proposals by members are accepted, even when they are not necessarily consistent with the latest NAM summit declaration. These factors combine to make it very difficult to adopt a coherent and effective NAM approach on many issues, and greatly impede the adjustment of collective NAM positions during the course of a Prep Com or Review Conference. They also help to explain why formal NAM papers tend to reflect the views articulated at prior NPT meetings and past NAM summits. This mode of decision-making contributes to what often is regarded by outside observers as outdated thinking and a lack of readiness to compromise on the part of NAM.

Although agility is not a notable NAM attribute, and continuity rather than dynamism tends to characterise the movement's policymaking on NPT matters, one should not assume that collective NAM positions significantly constrain the behaviour of individual NAM member and observer states. In fact, though national statements by members rarely depart from basic broad principles regarding nuclear disarmament and the inalienable right to peaceful uses, it is commonplace for members to stake out very different positions on specific topics that reflect their particular interests and priorities. This phenomenon was in evidence at the 2010 NPT Rev Con on such issues as the mandatory nature of the Additional Protocol, the importance of a Middle East NWFZ, and the effects of the NSG exemption for India.[88] Frequently, the common NAM position also exhibits a more pronounced ideological orientation than the views expressed in national statements on the same issue, a characteristic that may be explained in part by the informal understanding developed over many years among members that 'NAM consensus' is a vehicle for promoting a convergence of views – often shaped by a small number of more active members – without stifling the expression of different national positions on subjects of particular importance to some member states. Countries whose views diverge from the common NAM position actually may welcome the more extreme group stance as a means to promote their own more pragmatic national policies.[89]

One of the more surprising aspects of the 2010 NPT Rev Con was the inability of NAM members to effectively translate their shared nuclear-disarmament norms into creative, new approaches for eliminating nuclear weapons. Indeed, the movement often appeared to follow rather than lead the nuclear-disarmament charge by a number of European states on issues such as the Nuclear Weapons Convention and humanitarian law. On the one hand, this development may indicate a reorientation by NAM with respect to the priority that members attach to the issue of peaceful uses as opposed to disarmament. However, it also may highlight an opportunity for future cross-bloc cooperation on some important nuclear-disarmament issues.

It bears emphasising that NAM positions have evolved incrementally in the NPT context and that certain core principles have endured. Although the movement generally has difficulty in quickly changing course due to its diversity and mode of decision-making, on occasion it demonstrates more pragmatism and flexibility than one might anticipate. This apparent contradiction, evident in the support by NAM for the compromise 2010 Final Document, can be explained in part by shared norms and goals, which instil confidence among members in the basic contours of NAM policy. An informal but powerful principle of supporting (or at least not obstructing) other members in their pursuit of key objectives also helps to account for the manner in which non-Middle Eastern NAM states deferred to Egypt as NAM chair and a leading member of the Arab Group on the deal it was able to broker on the Middle East. Many NAM members and observers outside the Middle East may not have agreed fully with the resulting Final Document, but they recognised the importance some key members attached to the Middle East recommendations and were prepared to support the NAM chair and the conference president (from a NAM state) in forging at least a temporary NPT-related consensus. The ability of NAM to adopt a common position at the end of the Rev Con also probably reflects the fact that, while the principle of non-hierarchical decision-making provides an opportunity for many members to attempt to shape NAM positions, most members tend to defer to a relatively small number of NAM states. If this small grouping can reach agreement, their preferences are usually adopted by the collective.

CHAPTER THREE

Peaceful uses and beyond: NAM in Vienna

Peaceful uses of nuclear energy represent the third pillar of the Nuclear Non-proliferation Treaty, the last part of the bargain designed to ensure that states that forgo military nuclear programmes in accordance with Articles I and II of the treaty gain unfettered access to the atom's peaceful benefits. Article IV of the NPT recognises the inalienable right of states parties to develop and use nuclear energy for peaceful purposes and obligates them to facilitate the 'fullest possible exchange of equipment, materials and scientific and technological information for the peaceful uses of nuclear energy'. Furthermore, it specifies that parties with greater capabilities should cooperate in contributing 'to the further development of the applications of nuclear energy for peaceful purposes, especially in territories of non-nuclear-weapon States Party to the Treaty, with due consideration for the needs of the developing areas of the world'.

The issue of peaceful uses was not discussed during the treaty's negotiation until rather late in the process. According to Mohamed Shaker, it was only near the end of 1966 that Article IV was introduced into the draft text, at the request of the non-nuclear-weapons states.[1] The formulation of Article IV draws in particular on proposals from Mexico, Nigeria and Italy.[2] The section of the article emphasising the needs of developing countries reflected a Chilean proposal advanced at the First Committee session of the General Assembly in 1968.[3] Not surprisingly, the non-aligned states often highlight this reference to developing countries in their statements.

Promotion of peaceful nuclear uses and provision of assistance in this sphere are also part of the mandate of the International Atomic Energy Agency (IAEA), which was established in 1957 in Vienna. As Russell Leslie perceptively notes, NAM states' interpretation of the IAEA mission is 'analogous to [their] approach to discussions of the NPT'.[4] In other words, the three aspects of the agency's mandate also constitute a bargain, whereby states agree to subject their programmes to safeguards in exchange for technical cooperation and assistance in the use of nuclear energy and other nuclear applications. Such a view, Leslie argues, is fundamentally different from the Western paradigm, which holds safeguards to be intrinsically valuable, regardless of the state of assistance and cooperation.[5] These different paradigms affect the way the two groups approach the issues of rights and obligations, as well as the balance between different aspects of the IAEA's work. A failure to appreciate these differences by either the West or NAM can lead to scepticism about the sincerity of beliefs and motivations of the other party, a phenomenon all too evident in some of the debates surrounding the issue of peaceful uses of nuclear energy.

Peaceful uses and NAM priorities

The first several decades of the nuclear age were characterised by widespread fascination with the atom and a belief in the promise nuclear energy held for humankind. This sentiment, albeit in an extreme form, is captured in the following excerpt from a poem written in 1954 to commemorate the start-up of the first Soviet demonstration power reactor:

> Read,
> 　　Drink with your eyes the lines:
> The inevitable came true, the newest of
> 　　The miracles of the earth–
> The uranium forces
> 　　By electric current
> Over Soviet wires started to run! [...]
> Glory to those masters,
> Who, out of the fairy tales
> 　　Of the days gone,
> Created this reality.[6]

It was widely expected that nuclear energy would be cheap; its use would grow rapidly worldwide; and it would help developing countries to advance tremendously. This hope found expression as early as the Bandung Declaration in 1955, in the form of a paragraph welcoming the establishment of the IAEA, which was seen by the developing world as a potential boon to their economic advancement. Although early NAM summit documents did not devote much space to the issue, they too emphasised the potential benefits of peaceful nuclear technology for social and economic development.[7] The declaration adopted in 1976 at the Heads of State/Government Summit in Colombo, Sri Lanka, also mentioned the need for enhanced 'mutual cooperation in the production and use of nuclear energy' among NAM states.[8]

The 1979 Havana Declaration marked a significant increase in the attention given to the question of peaceful uses. For the first time a NAM declaration contained strong criticism of developed countries for placing 'obstacles ... in the way of transfers of technologies related to the peaceful uses of nuclear energy'. It also 'deplored the pressures and threats' allegedly directed against the developing states to prevent them from undertaking domestic nuclear-energy programmes.[9] Such language was probably a response to the creation and operation of two new nuclear export-control mechanisms (the Zangger Committee and the Nuclear Suppliers Group), the increased non-proliferation collaboration between the United States and the Soviet Union following India's 'peaceful' nuclear explosion in 1974, and the adoption of a new Non-proliferation Act in the United States in 1977 with very tough export-control restrictions. Another irritant for NAM at the time was the failure to realise the vision for a special international fund to finance nuclear-power projects in developing countries. As Shaker puts it, the special fund proposal was 'stillborn' because the countries whose support was necessary to establish and maintain the fund were not in a position to endorse it.[10]

Some of the formulations in the Havana Declaration – criticism of developed states for pressure and lack of assistance, defence of sovereign rights and concern about technology denial and the discriminatory nature of export-control regimes – became a regular feature of subsequent summit documents. Over time, specific references to the NPT were added and, in the most recent declarations, language can be found that differentiates between obligatory and voluntary safeguards and emphasises that multilateral nuclear-fuel arrangements should in no way limit the inalienable right to peaceful uses. These positions emerged in reaction to developments in the non-proliferation sphere and to new policy initiatives put forward in international forums, particularly in Vienna.

NAM at the IAEA

The principal venue for deliberation on matters related to peaceful uses is the Vienna-based International Atomic Energy Agency. As of 2012, it had 151 member states, the majority of which were developing countries. Unlike the NPT, IAEA membership includes nuclear-armed NAM members India and Pakistan, both of which are actively engaged in IAEA activities. The IAEA has two policymaking bodies: the all-inclusive General Conference (GC), which meets annually, and a 35-member Board of Governors, which typically meets at least five times a year.[11] In 2010–11, the IAEA Board included the following NAM members and observers, the first four of which serve in a de facto permanent capacity: Argentina, Brazil, India, South Africa, Cameroon, Chile, Ecuador, Jordan, Kenya, Mongolia, Niger, Pakistan, Peru, Singapore, Tunisia, the United Arab Emirates and Venezuela.[12] Collectively, NAM members and observers usually comprise slightly less than half of the Board of Governors.

As early as 1979, NAM states agreed that they 'should have a coordinated approach in the IAEA' to strengthen the role of developing countries.[13] Although the economic and technical interests of developing states in Vienna have traditionally been represented by the Group of 77, in 2003, at the particular urging of Iran, the movement also established a formal Vienna Chapter to address more political issues, including those in the nuclear sector.[14] Under an informal division of labour, NAM as a group only speaks on the agency's work related to one of the IAEA's six major programmes – verification and safeguards – while the G-77 addresses the extremely important matters of the agency's budget, nuclear power (for example, nuclear-fuel assurances), non-nuclear power applications, nuclear safety and security, and technical cooperation.[15] One of the most important and contentious issues at the IAEA is the annual negotiation of its budget and the allocation of resources to its different missions. As Leslie observes, the tension arises from the different approaches and interpretations of the IAEA 'statutory balance'.[16] NAM and the G-77 both seek greater equity in funding across the 'pillars' of the mandate, particularly between verification and assistance in peaceful uses, but it falls to the G-77 to make the case before the Board of Governors. At the board, the G-77 routinely objects to the fact that contributions to the Technical Cooperation Fund (TCF), used to finance a variety of assistance projects, are voluntary. Safeguards, in contrast, are funded through the regular budget, which is based on obligatory contributions by member states.[17] From the vantage point of the G-77 (and NAM), technical cooperation should be recognised as one of the agency's main activities, on a par with safeguards implementation, and funded accordingly. Therefore, many developing states see the inferior status of technical cooperation as contrary to the intent of the agency statute and Article IV of the NPT, which they believe provides for technical cooperation as a legal obligation. Moreover, although the dues most developing countries pay towards the agency's regular budget are small, they have the perception that they are paying for the implementation of safeguards, mostly in developed states, without getting adequate benefits in return.[18]

NAM and multinational fuel arrangements

Although less routine than the budgetary battle, extended debates related to assurances of nuclear fuel supply have occupied the G-77 and members of NAM since 2003. This dispute at the IAEA illustrates how easily well-intentioned plans can founder when parties fail to appreciate each other's basic interests and priorities. In this instance, a failure by nuclear supplier states to appreciate NAM positions and perspectives – even when they were clearly enunciated – led to years of fruitless debate and the expenditure of great effort and political capital with very little to show in return. A review of this case reveals that, while the West and Russia can usually get what they want at the board by wearing down NAM and peeling away its members' votes with various inducements, that process can be counterproductive and unnecessary.[19] A more proactive policy of consultation with key NAM/G-77 members early on and greater appreciation of their concerns might have led to a much more expeditious agreement that met the needs of both nuclear supplier and recipient states. An analysis of this case also suggests that, notwithstanding tough proclamations on fuel assurances in NAM summit and ministerial meetings, national positions among the non-aligned on fuel-assurance proposals are very mixed. They run the gamut from outright opposition to mild scepticism and approval and, in the cases of the United Arab Emirates and Kuwait, are even backed by sizable monetary contributions.

Proposals and reactions

Addressing the IAEA General Conference in September 2003, then-Director General Mohamed ElBaradei stated that in view of the possible growth of nuclear power worldwide and related proliferation concerns, it would be useful to examine '[the] merits and feasibility of multinational approaches to the management and disposal of spent fuel and radioactive waste'.[20] He elaborated on this statement in an op-ed in the *Economist* in which he proposed a three-part framework to deal with proliferation risks inherent in the spread of dual-use technologies and nuclear power: development of proliferation-resistant technologies, production of fissile materials only at facilities under multinational control, and multinational approaches to managing the back-end of the fuel cycle.[21] In 2004, ElBaradei appointed an Expert Group to examine the issue of multilateral nuclear fuel approaches (MNAs), and the group released its report in February 2005. A Special Event at the General Conference in 2006 was devoted to the same issue.

Russia and many Western countries – especially nuclear supplier states – enthusiastically welcomed the renewed interest in the idea of multilateral fuel arrangements, and were optimistic that the approach could be approved in a relatively short period of time. [22] By fall 2007, a dozen proposals had been put forward by national governments, groups of states, and non-governmental organisations, ranging from plans to create a back-up fuel reserve to establishing international control over all enrichment and reprocessing activities. [23] However, despite ElBaradei's concerted efforts to gain board support for several proposals, a decision was only taken in November 2009, shortly before he left his post. By a vote of 24 to eight with three abstentions, the IAEA Board of Governors authorised the establishment of a reserve of low-enriched uranium (LEU) in Russia. All but one of those dissenting votes were from NAM members and observers. [24] A year later, a second, related proposal to establish an LEU bank under IAEA auspices was postponed due to objections from the NAM and G-77. Addressing the board on behalf of both groups in June 2009, Cuba stated that it was premature to address the proposal and accept financial contributions towards the creation of the fuel bank. [25] A year later, however, a resolution on the establishment of an IAEA LEU bank passed with no votes against, though six board members abstained. [26] All six abstentions were from NAM members and observers. In March 2011, the board also voted on a proposal submitted by the UK on behalf of the EU countries, Russia and the United States. The UK proposal envisioned the conclusion of a supply-guarantee agreement between the nuclear supplier and recipient states, whereby the former would guarantee that the supply of LEU fuel would not be interrupted for non-commercial reasons. The IAEA would be a co-signatory of the agreement and confirm that the recipient state had comprehensive safeguards in place, was a party to the NPT, and met other requirements. The board adopted the proposal by a vote of 26 in favour, none against, and eight abstentions. Again, all the abstaining states were NAM members or observers (though several NAM members also voted in support of the proposal).[27]

NAM scepticism about MNAs should not have been a surprise to ElBaradei or the major proponents of the various fuel-assurance approaches when they were raised in Vienna. Countries such as Brazil, Egypt and South Africa had made clear their views about the subject at the 2005 NPT Review Conference.[28] There was also a marked difference in tone in the references to the MNAs by nuclear supplier states and those from the developing world at the Special Event and during the 2006 IAEA General Conference. Nuclear supplier states, as well as non-nuclear supplier states in the West, generally welcomed ElBaradei's initiative, described the idea as interesting and timely, and looked forward to the Special Event. NAM states, if they mentioned MNAs directly at all, expressed cautious interest but invariably added that no arrangement should come at the cost of further infringement of the right to peaceful uses and indigenous nuclear programmes, including the fuel cycle.[29] To many in NAM, the proposed multilateral arrangements represented a slippery slope towards technology denial. More concrete and technical objections were also expressed in response to specific proposals.

As indicated by Lance Joseph's review of the 2005 Expert Group report and reactions to it, many of the difficulties the MNA proposals encountered at the IAEA Board were foreseeable as early as 2005, during the drafting of the report. A participant in the Expert Group, Joseph observes that the director general's expectation of a report offering bold new ideas was far from met: 'What he received instead was yet another vapid document, full of everything – and nothing – and, in its recommendations, positively groaning with caution.'[30] The reasons for such caution were basically the same as those underlying the subsequent lukewarm response of countries to the proposals on multilateral fuel arrangements. As Joseph notes, experts in the group were not able to disassociate themselves from national positions and interests, or from what he calls the 'NPT review conference dogma' emphasising Article IV rights and unfulfilled obligations of the NWS.[31] This experience should have served as a warning that most IAEA member states – and not only NAM – were not ready to seriously consider the fundamental restructuring of fuel-supply frameworks that true multilateralisation requires. Instead, a number of states, primarily nuclear fuel suppliers, began to churn out proposals based on one or another of the different modalities identified in the report. Most of them focused on the least ambitious approach entailing the creation of 'fuel banks' and designating the IAEA as a guarantor of fuel supply and/or an arbiter in cases of disruption of existing supply due to political reasons.[32] NAM states, however, were not prepared to support even these limited arrangements.

Both of the projects approved by the IAEA Board of Governors in 2009 and 2010 involve the concept of a fuel bank. In the first case, a Russian reserve of 120 tonnes of low-enriched uranium hexafluoride is 'owned, operated and paid for by the Russian Federation'.[33] An IAEA member state can appeal to the agency in case its supply of nuclear fuel is disrupted for non-commercial reasons. The agency has the authority to decide if the state qualifies for back-up supply and can then request that Russia transfer the necessary amount of LEU, at the prevailing market price, to the appealing state. The conditions that recipient states must fulfill are very modest: they must have IAEA comprehensive safeguards in force and they cannot be under consideration by the Board of Governors with respect to safeguards implementation and compliance.[34] There are no requirements to forgo indigenous fuel-cycle capabilities, to bring into force the Additional Protocol or even to belong to the NPT. The second proposal involves the creation of an LEU bank under IAEA auspices and financed, at least initially, by member states and/or through other donations. As with the Russian proposal, states applying to receive uranium must have a comprehensive safeguards agreement in place, and 'the IAEA must conclude that there has been no diversion of declared material'.[35] The IAEA fuel bank is supposed to be used only as a supply of last resort if the recipient state cannot otherwise purchase fuel for non-technical and non-commercial reasons. The money for the start-up of the IAEA bank came from a pledge of $50 million from the Nuclear Threat Initiative in 2006 and subsequent contributions and pledges of $50m from the US government, $5m from Norway, €25m from the EU, $10m from the UAE and $10m from Kuwait.[36]

The fact that neither the Additional Protocol nor the renunciation of national fuel-cycle facilities is among the conditions of supply for the fuel-bank mechanism is the result of objections from developing countries, as well as the recognition by the director general that any significant conditionality would greatly impede the prospects for adoption at the board. According to Daniel Horner, 'in early articulations of fuel bank proposals, some supporters framed them to require recipients to forgo indigenous enrichment programmes', but these initiatives were met with stiff opposition from NAM states.[37] For example, in May 2006, six countries (France, Germany, the Netherlands, Russia, the United Kingdom and the United States) presented the board with a multi-tiered approach to assurance of fuel supply. It involved both commercial backup arrangements and establishment of LEU fuel reserves. Eligibility requirements for states to benefit from this mechanism included bringing into force the Additional Protocol and forgoing national 'sensitive' fuel-cycle activities, such as enrichment.[38] Many board members, including some Western states, thought it was premature to consider the proposal at that time. NAM states in particular objected to the requirements that they characterised as contradictory to Article IV of the NPT, and the six-nation concept was eventually replaced with other national proposals. Leading the charge against prompt endorsement of multilateral approaches were countries with existing nuclear programmes (for example, Brazil and South Africa) and Egypt, whose opposition to new limitations and associated verification measures is part of a broader policy that links adoption of any further non-proliferation measures to Israel's adherence to the NPT or, at a minimum, to progress on negotiation of a Middle East Nuclear-Weapons Free Zone.

The less-than-enthusiastic reaction of developing countries to the MNA proposals brought before the board was not all about politics and principled positions. All the governmental proposals, except the one from Austria, came from the current nuclear supplier states, and there was minimum engagement and consultation with the intended recipient – developing countries – prior to the submission of the proposals. NAM states objected to this process and insisted on both more dialogue and attentiveness to their views. The perceived urgency with which the director general sought board action on the MNA proposals and the push for these initiatives by the predominantly Western nuclear supplier states also made NAM members uneasy. To be sure, complaints about lack of dialogue and insufficient time for consideration were, in part, a strategy to delay any decision on the subject at the IAEA. At the same time, valid questions were raised about the perceived discriminatory nature of some of the proposals because of their focus on recipient rather than supplier states, as well as questions concerning the degree to which they were likely to have any meaningful impact on the problems they were designed to solve.[39] In addition, NAM states expressed substantive concerns about the logic of devoting time and resources to MNAs instead of their priority issues of peaceful nuclear applications in medicine, agriculture and other spheres.

While the MNAs were marketed as an idea that made sense economically and from a non-proliferation standpoint, as well as enhancing energy security of importing states, in reality, most proposals did not directly address any specific or immediate needs. The insistence that MNAs not distort the existing market, which the supplier states argued worked 'just fine', limited the scope of potential arrangements and conditions under which states could apply for access to the fuel bank. Moreover, the adopted proposals do not constitute a sustainable assurance of supply, but are backup arrangements for extreme cases. A non-market, non-technical, politically motivated disruption that is not related to a dispute about safeguards implementation, from the NAM states' perspective, is an unlikely hypothetical situation. Brazil and other countries have therefore characterised the fuel backup proposals as a solution in search of a problem. Although the original MNA initiative was clearly designed with non-proliferation considerations in mind, this focus soon was overtaken by commercial considerations. The minimalist conditions attached to the measures ultimately adopted by the board are unlikely to have much impact from a non-proliferation standpoint.

Finally, the debate on multilateral arrangements suffered from unfortunate timing and the convergence of other trends in nuclear disarmament and non-proliferation. By 2004, when the Expert Group started its work, the 'decade of estrangement' was well under way and mutual grievances were mounting over unfulfilled commitments related to the 1995 and 2000 NPT Conferences, such as a zone free from WMD in the Middle East and implementation of the '13 Practical Steps', as well as various proliferation breaches. In February 2004, US President George W. Bush, speaking at the National Defense University, presented a new, seven-step non-proliferation initiative designed to curb global proliferation. Step four of the proposal sought to close the 'loop-hole' contained in Article IV of the NPT while ensuring 'reliable access at reasonable cost to fuel for civilian reactors'.[40] Bush stated that members of the Nuclear Suppliers Group 'should refuse to sell enrichment and reprocessing equipment and technologies' to states that did not already have operational fuel-cycle facilities.[41] Thus, the concept of fuel assurances – multilateral or otherwise – became inextricably linked to technology denial, reinterpretation of the NPT and export-control policies of the NSG, which the developing states have always viewed with deep suspicion. It also did not help that the entire speech preceding the outline of the seven steps was devoted to the threats of nuclear terrorism, operation of illicit networks and nuclear ambitions of 'rogue' states. In this context, subsequent arguments that MNAs were not meant to infringe on anyone's rights or that developing countries were not collectively the target of the initiative rang hollow.

Notwithstanding the centrality of the issue of MNAs at the IAEA for more than half a decade, the medium-term outlook for multilateral fuel-supply mechanisms is not promising. The limited, reserve fuel-bank arrangements are currently not required by the market and do not directly resolve any immediate proliferation problems. The establishment of truly multilateral fuel-cycle facilities under international control – as envisioned in the early suggestions (dating back to the Baruch Plan of 1946) and the 2007 Austrian proposal – is, apparently, an idea whose time has not yet come.[42] A full multilateralisation of the fuel cycle, with abolition of purely nationally controlled facilities everywhere, would require the support of existing nuclear suppliers, including (most importantly) the nuclear-weapons states. Such support is unlikely to be forthcoming any time soon. Moreover, establishment of an exclusive MNA would necessitate the redefinition of the exercise of Article IV rights, which neither NAM nor the West is prepared to undertake.

NAM and Iran's nuclear programme

Since 2003, the question of peaceful use has become deeply entangled with the case of Iran's nuclear programme.[43] This linkage has occurred thanks both to the skilful manoeuvring of Iranian diplomats and the Western push to strengthen IAEA verification capabilities and limit the diffusion of fuel-cycle technology. The non-aligned states' reluctance to exert pressure on Iran or condemn its violations of safeguards obligations has fuelled Western speculation and suspicions about NAM's stance on non-proliferation. NAM states, for their part, have resented attempts to turn voluntary measures into legal obligations and worried that non-proliferation actions directed at one state effectively limit the right to peaceful uses of nuclear energy for all. This sentiment is reflected in NAM summit and ministerial meeting documents, working papers and statements at IAEA and NPT forums.[44] On the other hand, the movement does not speak with a unified voice on this issue, and several NAM states have voted in favour of IAEA Board of Governors and UN Security Council resolutions finding Iran in non-compliance with its safeguards obligations, requesting that it suspend its enrichment and heavy-water-related activities and ultimately imposing sanctions.

The principle

NAM views on the case of Iran's compliance with agency safeguards did not form in isolation from other contemporaneous disarmament and non-proliferation developments. An atmosphere of disenchantment with and distrust of the United States and its nuclear allies, fuelled by their failure to deliver fully on the promises they made at the 1995 and 2000 NPT Conferences, provided the backdrop against which NAM positions at the IAEA on Iran were formulated. The Bush administration's efforts to promote restrictions on the spread of sensitive fuel-cycle technologies while simultaneously moving to grant a nuclear-weapons possessor outside the NPT (India) an exemption was correctly seen as an 'exceptionalist approach' to non-proliferation and irritated many of the non-nuclear NAM states.[45] Fresh memories of the United States and Britain invading Iraq under the pretext of non-proliferation enforcement, after dismissing UNMOVIC's conclusions about the country's alleged WMD programmes, also contributed to NAM scepticism of Western accusations. Not surprisingly in this context, NAM countries were wary of joining in the Western condemnation of Iran for fear that the initiative was politically motivated by a desire for additional regime change.

Such suspicions allowed Iranian diplomats and supporters to argue that the case presented against them was part of a larger assault on the rights of developing countries that required a united and forceful NAM response. In September 2003, the issue was taken up at the NAM Ministerial Meeting in New York, during the UN General Assembly session. The declaration adopted by the foreign ministers of NAM countries welcomed 'the increased cooperation' between the IAEA and Iran and reaffirmed previously voiced reservations on several operative paragraphs of the September 2003 board resolution on Iran.[46] The November 2005 NAM Troika

Communiqué devoted an impressive five paragraphs to the Iranian nuclear issue, reaffirming, among other things, that 'States Parties' choices and decisions, including that of the Islamic Republic of Iran, in the field of peaceful uses of nuclear technology and its fuel-cycle policies, should be respected'.[47] In 2006, two NAM statements specifically on Iran were adopted, one at the Ministerial Conference in Malaysia and one at the Heads of State/Government Summit in Cuba.[48] An additional 'Statement on Iran's Nuclear Issue' was issued at the Ministerial Conference in Tehran in July 2008.[49] None of these statements contained any criticism of Iran's actions and only encouraged Iran to 'urgently continue to cooperate' with the IAEA. The newly established Vienna Chapter of NAM also assumed an active stance on the issue of Iran's nuclear activities and made it a practice from the early days of the dispute to regularly address the board on this subject.[50] For the most part, its statements expressed support for Iran's right to peaceful uses of nuclear energy and development of indigenous capabilities, emphasised Iran's cooperation with the agency, and called for a diplomatic solution to the controversy.

The particulars

Though NAM countries normally prefer to present a united front and are wary of bringing an issue to a vote on the board where they are usually outnumbered, one can discern that major differences of opinion within NAM have existed since the beginning of the Iran nuclear saga. They became more pronounced and evident after 2005. In private conversations, NAM diplomats make no secret of the lack of consensus in the movement on Iran's nuclear programme, in spite of official NAM statements that papered over these differences. Between September 2003 and September 2005, the IAEA Board of Governors adopted seven resolutions on safeguards implementation in Iran, all of them without a vote, but with language far softer than that preferred by the United States and European countries. Most significantly, during this time NAM states on the Board successfully resisted the introduction of firm deadlines for 'final conclusions' about the case into the texts of the resolutions and, along with Russia, prevented a referral to the UN Security Council.[51] However, in September 2005, the IAEA Board voted to find that Iran's actions constituted non-compliance 'in the context of Article XII.C' of the IAEA Statute,[52] and in February 2006, the board referred the case to the Security Council. Five NAM members and one observer voted in favour of the September 2005 resolution, while six members and two observers voted for the February 2006 resolution.[53]

The issue of the movement's response to the Iranian programme is among the very few topics related to NAM nuclear politics that have received scholarly attention. For example, in an article on 'International Responses to Iranian Nuclear Defiance: The Non-Aligned Movement and the Issue of Non-Compliance', Tanya Ogilvie-White examines the evolution of NAM's stance between 2003 and 2006.[54] One of the central questions she raises is whether a 'sudden collapse of NAM unity' in 2005–06 was indicative of a broader trend – that of greater convergence of views on non-proliferation between Western states and those of NAM.[55] She points out that many developing countries at the time thought that defection from a common NAM stance over Iran was 'a one-off event', resulting from 'pressure and threats', but that this view was proven wrong by subsequent votes at the IAEA and the United Nations Security Council. This development, she argues, was evidence of an emerging split within NAM in terms of positions on stronger non-proliferation measures and their enforcement, although the majority remained deeply suspicious about the West's motivations.[56] NAM states' votes on the six UN Security

Table 1. **UN Security Council Resolutions on Iran's nuclear programme, 2006–10, with voting record**

UNSC Resolution	In favour	Against	Abstain
1696 (2006) Demands that Iran suspend enrichment-related and reprocessing activities by 31 August; Calls on Iran to implement the Additional Protocol and other transparency measures; Endorses the proposals by the P5+1 (China, France, Russia, UK, US and Germany) for a long-term comprehensive arrangement to provide assurance about Iran's nuclear programme	Argentina,* China, Denmark, **DRC**, France, **Ghana**, Greece, Japan, **Peru**, Russia, Slovakia, United Kingdom, **United Republic of Tanzani**a, United States	Qatar	None
1737 (2006) Reiterates previous demands; demands that Iran suspend heavy-water-related projects; calls on Iran to ratify the Additional Protocol; Decides that states shall 'prevent the supply, sale or transfer' to Iran of items, materials, goods, technology, etc. that can contribute to its enrichment, reprocessing and heavy-water-related activities; Imposes travel bans and financial sanctions against designated individuals and entities; Puts restrictions on IAEA technical cooperation with Iran	Argentina, China, Denmark, **DRC**, France, **Ghana**, Greece, Japan, **Peru**, **Qatar**, Russia, Slovakia, United Kingdom, **Tanzania**, United States	None	None
1747 (2007) Reiterates previous demands; Expands the list of designated individuals and entities under sanctions; Imposes limitations on arms trade with Iran; Calls upon states to report on the implementation of the resolution to the committee established under UNSCR 1737 (2006); Calls on UN members not to enter into new commitments for grants or concessional loans to Iran; Commits to suspend sanctions if Iran suspends enrichment-related and reprocessing activities	Belgium, China, **DRC**, France, **Ghana**, **Indonesia**, Italy, **Panama**, **Peru**, **Qatar**, Russia, Slovakia, **South Africa**, United Kingdom, United States	None	None
1803 (2008) Reiterates previous demands; Welcomes the work plan concluded by the IAEA and Iran to clarify outstanding issues; Adds new lists of designated individuals and entities; Calls on states to inspect cargo on vehicles owned or operated by certain Iranian entities and report to the committee under UNSCR 1737 (2006); Prohibits the trade with Iran in certain designated items that can contribute to its nuclear and missile programmes; Imposes additional financial sanctions; Encourages further efforts to achieve a negotiated solution; Commits to suspend sanctions if Iran suspends enrichment-related and reprocessing activities	Belgium, **Burkina Faso**, China, *Costa Rica*, Croatia, France, Italy, **Libya**, **Panama**, Russia, **South Africa**, United Kingdom, United States, **Vietnam**	None	Indonesia

Table 1. **UN Security Council Resolutions on Iran's nuclear programme, 2006–10, with voting record**

UNSC Resolution	In favour	Against	Abstain
1835 (2008) Reaffirms previous resolutions; Reaffirms commitment to achieve a negotiated solution	Belgium, **Burkina Faso**, China, *Costa Rica*, Croatia, France, **Indonesia**, Italy, **Libya**, **Panama**, Russia, **South Africa**, United Kingdom, United States, **Vietnam**	None	None
1929 (2010) Reaffirms previous demands, prohibits Iran from constructing new enrichment facilities; Demands that Iran comply with relevant IAEA BoG and UNSC resolutions, and its Safeguards Agreement; Reaffirms arms trade and other limitations imposed by preceding resolutions; Calls on states to prevent the provision of financial services, assets or resources if they are believed to contribute to 'Iran's proliferation-sensitive nuclear activities'; Calls on states to prohibit the establishment of new branches, etc. of Iranian banks on their territory, and establishment by their financial institutions of branches, etc. on Iranian territory; Establishes a group of experts to support the work of the committee established pursuant to UNSCR 1737 (2006)	Austria, Bosnia and Herzegovina, China, France, **Gabon**, Japan, *Mexico*, **Nigeria**, Russian Federation, **Uganda**, United Kingdom, United States	*Brazil*, Turkey	Lebanon

NAM members at the time are printed in **bold**, and observers in *italics*.

*Argentina rejoined NAM as an observer in 2009.

Council resolutions concerning Iran's nuclear programme would seem to confirm this observation. Between 2006 and 2010, most NAM states on the council voted in favour of resolutions that requested Iran to suspend enrichment activities and ratify the Additional Protocol, and imposed sanctions ranging from restrictions on the nuclear and missile programmes to an arms embargo, asset freeze and other financial measures. The table above summarises the voting records for all the UNSC resolutions on Iran.

While the votes in the Security Council reflect the growing displeasure among NAM states about Iran's failure to fully cooperate with the agency, a number of these countries also had to keep other factors in mind when casting a vote. Aside from principled positions, pragmatic considerations linked to each state's political and economic relations with the United States and the EU influenced the decisions. Finally, an examination of the explanation of votes reveals that, while many delegations supported the Western-backed actions on Iran, they were keen to emphasise that the Iranian case should not be the basis for limiting other states' choices to exercise their inalienable right to peaceful uses of nuclear energy.

The crucial vote: a closer look

the September 2005 vote was very significant in the development of the IAEA Board's handling of the Iranian case and NAM participation in it. However, a more nuanced interpretation is in order. Rather than representing a 'sudden collapse' of NAM unity, the vote revealed the previously existing differences in positions and the weakened ability of the movement to act as a bloc. Before September 2005, NAM states on the Board, acting in consort, were able to negotiate with their European and American counterparts to soften the language of draft resolutions so that they could be adopted without a vote. South Africa in particular took the initiative to table alternative drafts and to reconcile the differences. Malaysia, NAM chair at the time, facilitated the negotiation of common NAM positions. The resulting texts were not always satisfactory to all, and some NAM delegations expressed reservations, but they still supported the consensus, upholding the proverbial 'spirit of Vienna'. Furthermore, it would be wrong to characterise the NAM stance at the time as a refusal to recognise any wrongdoing on Iran's part. On the contrary, NAM members and observers on the board expressed (in their national capacities) varying degrees of concern and underscored the need for Iran to cooperate fully. But they were united in opposing a swift referral of the case to the Security Council, perhaps fearful that such a step could lead to military action. The invasion of

Iraq had been undertaken only shortly before, in 2003, and the scenario of 'Iran is next' did not then appear to be completely beyond the realm of possibilities.

The run-up to the board resolution of September 2005, however, involved a different dynamic. In August 2005, the negotiations between Iran and the three EU states (or E3, comprising France, Germany and the UK) that had been initiated in autumn 2003 broke down.[57] Iran demanded that the E3 submit its proposal for a long-term cooperation framework as envisioned in the Paris Agreement and rejected the submitted draft as unsatisfactory. It then proceeded to restart uranium conversion activities at Esfahan, thereby breaking the suspension that had been in place fitfully since November 2003. This triggered a special meeting of the IAEA Board in August and the adoption of a resolution that called on Iran to renew the suspension of uranium conversion.[58] Introduction of a new draft resolution by France, Germany and the UK at the September Board meeting, therefore, seemed to catch NAM by surprise. NAM delegates protested that they had not been properly consulted or informed sufficiently in advance that a draft would be tabled.

In spite of protestations and appeals to consider the draft at a later time, the co-sponsors demanded action on the resolution 24 hours after its introduction, which left NAM as a group with no time to consolidate its position or revise the text. Delegations had barely enough time to receive instructions from their respective capitals. The resolution that opened the door for the referral to the Security Council was thus steamrolled through the board and forced the divergences in NAM views into the open. More importantly, it demonstrated to NAM that its Western counterparts were no longer interested in preserving consensus if it meant compromising on the text, which weakened the movement's bargaining leverage.

As it turned out, NAM was unable to forge internal consensus and vote as a bloc on this issue. The longer-term impact of this board action, however, was the empowerment of hardliners within the Vienna Chapter, as it reduced incentives to moderate their tone and deprived other diplomats of the argument that a less confrontational approach would ensure that NAM views are given proper consideration.

The divergent votes cast by NAM states not only reflected their national positions on verification and compliance per se, but were also indicative of a variety of factors and relationships that influence individual states' decisions. India, for example, while appealing along with others for more time and greater consideration to be given to NAM positions, nonetheless voted for the resolution. One might argue that it was a sign of India 'buying into' the non-proliferation regime and the Western view of it – or was simply part of its disassociation from NAM through a budding 'strategic relationship' with the United States and the pursuit of the bilateral nuclear deal. Abstentions by some of the key states, such as Brazil and South Africa, did not signify a lack of strong views on the matter, as both had serious reservations about the manner in which the resolution was introduced, the urgency for action, and its broader implications for the regime. At the same time, these states were reluctant to cast votes against the resolution, in part because of their concerns about Iran's nuclear programme but also due to important foreign-policy considerations besides non-proliferation, such as their relations with the United States. In the Board of Governors, a body that customarily operates by consensus, a 'no' vote is a very powerful negative statement indicative of a fundamental disagreement. Between 2005 and 2009, with one exception, only the three states in open ideological confrontation with the United States – Cuba, Syria and Venezuela – voted in this fashion at the board. The one exception was Malaysia, which voted against a Board of Governors' resolution on Iran in November 2009, but its vote appeared to be based on a misunderstanding within the delegation rather than a national position.[59] Still, the consensus spirit of Vienna was weakened, and since September 2005, voting has become a more common modality for decision-making at the board – both on the Iranian nuclear programme and on other issues, such as assurances of fuel supply.

NAM positions: major strands

On the basis of different national statements by NAM parties, explanations of their votes, and personal conversations by the authors with diplomats, one can discern several strands of thinking on the Iranian nuclear case. For many NAM countries, the issue of Iran's nuclear activities is not a pressing national concern. They are not particularly involved in nuclear issues and do not have sufficient expertise on nuclear matters to engage actively in debates on Iran. A number of these states, as well as those with greater expertise, accept the position that the right to peaceful nuclear uses is inalienable, that the IAEA is the competent authority to draw conclusions about compliance with safeguards obligations, and that the crisis should be resolved peacefully. Among those that are more involved and have stronger opinions, however, differences exist on their assessment of the implications of the Iranian nuclear programme.

Some NAM countries, for example, are seriously concerned by Iran's activities and share the prevailing Western view that non-proliferation verification measures need to be enhanced both with respect to Iran and more generally. They do not necessarily view new measures, such as the Additional Protocol, as impinging on their right to peaceful uses of nuclear energy, but resist attempts to permanently limit their choices in terms of an indigenous fuel cycle. Examples of these states include Singapore, Thailand and Chile. On occasion these states and others that appear poised to defect from the NAM consensus reportedly are reminded by other NAM members of the superior bloc cohesion within the EU and the need to approximate the solidarity of its members.[60] A related, though somewhat muted, sentiment within NAM is annoyance that Iran continues to use the movement and its solidarity to the detriment of those whom it routinely calls brotherly nations. For these countries, Iran's behaviour legitimises those who want to limit the right to peaceful use, an action that is contrary to NAM's interests.

Egypt and other, but not all, Arab states view the question of the Iranian nuclear programme and safeguards compliance primarily in a regional context and through the prism of Israel's nuclear status. They therefore frame the problem in political terms; Egypt indicated early on that resolution of the Iranian matter would require that it be addressed in the broader context of the Middle East security equation. Egypt has its eyes on the prize – the establishment of an NWFZ in the Middle East and Israel's disarmament – and is loathe to let other issues detract from those goals. While Western states have argued that Iranian non-compliance and the lack of resolution of the crisis stand in the way of progress toward a Middle East NWFZ, Egypt is not prepared to openly endorse this notion, at least not until comparable pressure is put on Israel by the same Western states. In contrast, the Arab Gulf states, such as the UAE, tend to be more alarmed by the potential threat posed to their own security by Iran, and are also influenced by pragmatic economic considerations related to their developing nuclear ties with the United States.

Brazil, along with other Latin American NAM countries – except Cuba and Venezuela – never hesitated to call on Iran to comply with its non-proliferation obligations and extend the necessary cooperation to the IAEA. Brazil's main concern, however, was that the Iranian case not become a precedent and pretext to impose new obligations on other non-nuclear-weapon states, such as the proposal to make the Additional Protocol a requirement under Article III of the NPT. As Brazil has put it, it cannot accept the logic that catching a cheater or two is reason enough to impose new rules on everyone.[61] Brazil is certainly not alone in this view, as many in NAM, especially between 2004 and 2006, believed they were being collectively punished for one state's transgressions. These countries also emphasise the importance of balance in the NPT, arguing that a strong response to non-compliance in non-proliferation also requires equally earnest implementation of the other two pillars of the treaty – disarmament and assistance in peaceful uses.

A slightly different stance on Iran has been staked out by South Africa. While it shares Brazil's views on the need for balance of obligations and rights with respect to peaceful uses, it has also raised concerns about the relationship between the agency and the Security Council and their respective roles in the non-proliferation regime. As a de facto permanent repre-sentative on the IAEA Board of Governors but not on the Security Council, South Africa has argued that the authority of the board should not be undermined by excessive referral of matters within its domain to the Security Council. In its view, the Security Council is prone to be used as a political tool in targeting particular countries rather than strengthening the non-proliferation regime. In 2007, while voting in favour of UN Security Council Resolution 1747 on Iran, the South African delegation stated that:

South Africa has always been very clear, as a matter of principle, that the Security Council must remain within its mandate of addressing threats to international peace and security. If the sponsors of the resolution were convinced that the Iranian programme was a threat to international peace, then the Security Council should have been asked to take a decision on a draft that would have concentrated on that, and not to act as if the Iranian Government itself posed a threat to international peace and security.[62]

In 2008, South Africa again pointed out the impression that the verification work done by the IAEA appeared 'virtually irrelevant to the sponsors of this draft resolution' at the Security Council.[63]

Over time, the South African position on the appropriate roles of the Security Council and the IAEA Board has gained sympathy beyond Vienna and outside the context of the Iranian crisis. A broad sector of NAM diplomats, as well as some from non-NAM countries, has expressed concern that the Security Council has begun to legislate on matters beyond its mandate. Although their claims are widely disputed by others, they cite as examples UN Security Council Resolutions 1540 and 1887, and observe that broad-based, multilateral and negotiated frameworks are being replaced by ad hoc arrangements – adopted by 'like-minded' states or, at best, the UN Security Council – that almost invariably focus on non-proliferation and nuclear security.

The November 2011 report of the IAEA Director General to the board might have opened a new chapter in the controversy surrounding Iran's nuclear programme, although at the time of writing, it was too early to judge its effect on NAM. The report contains a 13-page annex that addresses the so-called 'possible military dimensions' to Iran's nuclear programme, with findings based on intelligence provided by some of the member states and IAEA's own verification work. The annex alleges that, at least until the end of 2003, Iran engaged in a range of research activities applicable to nuclear-weapon development.[64] Preceded by considerable hype in the Western media about its likely findings and conclusions, the restricted report was leaked to the press the day of its submission to the board and provoked a flurry of commentary about its implications.[65] While most observers and policymakers in the West focused on discussion that Iran had, or possibly still has, a nuclear-weapons programme, Russia criticised the timing of the report and some of its findings. The NAM Vienna Chapter held a long emergency meeting, at which Iran distributed a six-page Questions and Answers document, which focused on questions related to nuclear materials and implementation of comprehensive safeguards, and suggested that the IAEA was being manipulated by 'some countries'.[66] Aside from concerns about Iran's programme in particular, at least some NAM members are likely to question the IAEA's authority to investigate non-nuclear activities of a state without an Additional Protocol in force, the use of intelligence provided by other member states, and the extent to which the timing of the report was indeed influenced by the United States and its European allies.

The preceding analysis of IAEA efforts to address Iran's compliance with its safeguards obligations indicates that NAM on occasion speaks with multiple voices on the Board. This demonstration of a tendency to place considerations of national interest above those of NAM solidarity, however, should not be interpreted to mean that most members of the movement have abandoned their strong commitment to the principle of the inalienable right to peaceful uses or have fully embraced Western non-proliferation priorities. Regardless of how much discomfort Iran's nuclear defiance causes them, and despite the importance they may attach to non-proliferation, most NAM parties would not give up or reinterpret the inalienable right to peaceful uses in order to 'prevent another Iran'. Moreover, the majority of NAM view Iran (and Syria, for that matter) as a troubling and serious, but still special case, and dispute the notion that the world would be made safer simply by keeping sensitive nuclear technologies out of the hands of developing countries.

INC resolution controversy

No issue has been more divisive at the IAEA in recent years than the subject of Israeli nuclear capabilities and the Resolution on the Application of IAEA Safeguards in the Middle East. Heated disagreement over these two agenda items at the General Conference has not only derailed the oft-cited consensus 'spirit of Vienna', it has also tested the unity of NAM and its power as a voting bloc at the agency.

The vote and adoption of the Israeli Nuclear Capability (INC) Resolution in 2009, which called on Israel to place all its nuclear facilities under IAEA safeguards, might have come as a surprise to many observers. However, the issue has a long history. The compromise approach that had worked for more than a decade began to falter in 2006. The NAM Vienna Chapter's involvement in an official capacity in what had previously been an Arab states' issue resulted from the growing activism of NAM at the IAEA, the appeal to many NAM members of what had long been a core principle and shared norm, and the personal characteristics of several key NAM diplomats in Vienna.

INC: the prehistory

'Israeli Nuclear Capabilities and Threat' had been a General Conference agenda item for several sessions in the 1980s, and a resolution on the subject was adopted every year between 1987 and 1991.[67] The resolution called on Israel to place all its nuclear facilities under IAEA safeguards, urged the supplier states to require full-scope safeguards as a condition of supply of nuclear materials and equipment to Israel, and requested the director general to 'consult with the Israeli authorities on the implementation of this resolution' and report to the General Conference (GC) accordingly.[68] In 1992, however, in light of the Madrid Peace Conference and then on-going Arms Control and Regional Security (ACRS) process, it was agreed that in order to maintain goodwill and cooperation of all involved parties, the item would not be discussed, and no resolution was introduced.[69] The compromise also entailed the adoption, without a vote, of a resolution on the application of IAEA safeguards in the Middle East – a compromise achieved at the price of not mentioning the NPT in the text of the resolution.[70] Expressing concern about the presence of unsafeguarded nuclear activities in the Middle East, the resolution reaffirmed the need for states in the region to apply comprehensive IAEA safeguards to all their nuclear activities and further called on them to take steps towards the establishment of a NWFZ in the Middle East.[71]

The item 'Israeli Nuclear Capabilities and Threat' did not reappear on the GC agenda until 1998, when the Arab Group requested that the item be re-inscribed on the agenda, citing the stagnation of the peace process, the Resolution on the Middle East adopted by the 1995 NPT Review and Extension Conference, and the negotiation of the Model Additional Protocol that strengthened the IAEA's safeguards system.[72] The Arab states, however, did not introduce a resolution on Israeli nuclear capabilities (INC), and until 2006, the subject was covered by a statement from the president of the General Conference. As part of the compromise package, the resolution on application of safeguards in the Middle East continued to be adopted by consensus, but starting in 1995, it specifically invited all 'concerned states' to join the NPT.

During the aforementioned period, the INC and Middle East more generally were not issues that pitted NAM against the West/US at the General Conference. NAM was not even formally represented in Vienna until 2003, and the non-aligned members of the agency did not appear to have a unified position. While there was always broad support for the establishment of a NWFZ in the Middle East, until the mid-1990s several NAM states and observers were not in a position to support the call for Israel to accede to the NPT, as they had not joined the treaty themselves.[73] By and large, the issue was regional, championed by the Arab states and Iran. This situation changed, however, in 2007.

Deep divisions: 2006–09

The compromise and consensus broke down in 2006, when the Arab states tabled, for the first time since 1991, an INC resolution along with the usual resolution on safeguards in the Middle East. To understand what transpired at the General Conference with respect to the INC, one first must appreciate several basic procedural steps that IAEA members can take. Firstly, any member state can propose the addition of an item such as the INC to the agenda for the General Conference (something the Arab Group has done routinely since 2006).[74] Secondly, during the discussion of an agenda item at the conference any delegate can propose adjournment of the debate (a 'no action motion'). Under Rule 59 of the Rules and Procedures of the General Conference, a proposal to adjourn the debate must be put to a vote immediately, and if a majority of delegations present votes in favour, the chair closes debate on the issue and moves on to the next item on the agenda. Such a parliamentary procedure, employed several times by Canada with respect to the INC, can be adopted before any state makes a statement or, alternatively, after statements are made and a debate transpires. Another option is for a vote to take place on the item if a draft resolution is introduced. Typically, NAM as a group takes a formal position regarding the addition of items to the Agenda and the no-action motion, but does not take a stance as a group if a vote is necessitated.

In 2006, Canada successfully introduced an adjournment-of-debate motion in regard to the INC, a manoeuvre that appears to have taken the Arab Group – and NAM in general – by surprise. By a simple majority, the conference decided not to bring the INC resolution forward for a vote. This decision reflected the belief among the Western and several NAM states that the issue of Israel's nuclear capability is too political for the IAEA and should be addressed elsewhere. At the same time, according to some diplomats, the adjournment vote also benefited from the absence of many delegations from smaller NAM states and confusion among some of those present in the room about the procedure.[75]

A direct and immediate consequence of re-introducing the INC agenda item was Israel's call for a vote on the Middle East Safeguards Resolution, which previously had been the subject of consensus action, and the text of which was identical to that of preceding years.[76] The resolution passed with a large majority in favour, but both Israel and the United States voted against it. Subsequently the two Middle East agenda items generated increased acrimony among states and also affected NAM politics.

The Arab states' decision to re-introduce the INC resolution in 2006 appears to be tied both to the deteriorating situation in the Middle East and the failure to reach any substantive agreements at the 2005 NPT Rev Con, including, most importantly from the Arab perspective, progress in implementing the 1995 resolution. In summer 2006, Israel inflicted massive destruction in southern Lebanon in its war against Hizbullah, and in July that year

Secretary-General of the League of Arab States Amr Moussa declared the peace process 'dead'.[77] As the United States at the time refused to criticise Israel's reaction (to Hizbullah's kidnapping of an Israeli Defense Force soldier) as disproportionate, the atmosphere at the General Conference in September was tense. The US vote against the Middle East safeguards resolution was seen as further evidence by the Arab states that the Bush administration was not interested in advancing implementation of the 1995 NPT Middle East Resolution and would support Israel unconditionally. US votes in other international bodies at this time were consistent with this interpretation, and 2006 may be viewed as a low point as far as US support for multilateral disarmament and non-proliferation matters is concerned.[78]

In 2007 the Arab states were unable to garner support for tabling the INC resolution or securing a presidential statement on the matter. Instead, they chose to amend the Middle East Safeguards Resolution. Introduced by Egypt, the two amendments 'called on the States of the region not to develop, produce, test or otherwise acquire nuclear weapons' and 'urged the nuclear-weapon States to assist in establishing a nuclear-weapon-free zone in the Middle East'.[79] The resolution was again put to vote and passed with much less support than before; all the EU and associated states abstained, along with six NAM states, five of which were African.

Matters deteriorated further in 2008, plunging the General Conference into a lengthy and controversial amendment process. Israel introduced three amendments to the Middle East Safeguards Resolution, two of which were adopted by a majority vote: a call for states in the region to comply with their safeguards obligations and an amendment emphasising 'the importance of the peace process in the Middle East in promoting mutual confidence and security in the region, including the establishment of a NWFZ'.[80] Arab states, following the initiative of the Algerian ambassador, countered by introducing an additional operative paragraph calling on all states in the region to accede to the NPT (Operative Paragraph 2). The paragraph was adopted by a vote, but the next proposal, which would have removed the conditionality between the peace process and the NWFZ, was defeated. In an attempt to offset the second Israeli amendment, the Algerian ambassador proposed a new paragraph that would have read, 'emphasizes the importance of the peace process and the establishment of a NWFZ in the Middle East in promoting mutual confidence and security in the region'.[81] After much confusion about the application of rules of procedure, the conference voted not to consider the Algerian amendment. The Middle East safeguards resolution as a whole was finally adopted (with a separate vote on Operative Paragraph 2), but by then the 'spirit of Vienna' was a distant memory. Consideration of the draft INC resolution, tabled by the Arab Group, was once again blocked by a successful procedural no-action motion initiated by Canada.

In an effort to break this escalating cycle of discord at the agency and to forge consensus on the Middle East Safeguards Resolution, Egypt, Israel, the United States and the EU engaged in intensive consultations in advance of the autumn 2009 General Conference.[82] When the draft came up for consideration at the plenary on 17 September, it appeared that the parties were close to an agreement – at least there was no repetition of the previous years' amendment exercises on the conference floor. The resolution was adopted by vote, but with minimum controversy and with no votes against. It was peculiar, however, that after thanking all the negotiating parties in his national capacity, the Egyptian representative then took the floor on behalf of NAM and delivered a statement that was completely different in tone, quoting at length the 2009 Sharm El-Sheikh NAM Summit Declaration and condemning

Israel. The next day, speaking on behalf of NAM in support of the draft INC Resolution (introduced for the Arab states by Lebanon), he again quoted the same paragraph from the Sharm El-Sheikh document.

In 2009, the Arab states conducted more intense lobbying among NAM members, whose united stance contributed to the defeat of the Canadian procedural no-action motion by a comfortable majority. As the chair of the Non-Aligned Movement at the time, Egypt was in a better position to mobilise NAM support for the Arab initiatives. The Arab states also succeeded in persuading more delegations to be present in the room at the time of the vote on the INC Resolution, which was adopted by a narrow margin of 49 in favour, 45 against, and 16 abstentions.[83] None of the NAM members and observers voted against, but several abstained, including a number of Latin American states, such as Brazil, Chile, Mexico and Peru. The representative of Lebanon, speaking on behalf of the Arab states members of the IAEA, specifically thanked NAM, the African Group and the Organisation of the Islamic Conference for defeating the no-action motion. Still, all the states that abstained on the resolution, except the Holy See, were NAM members or observers, which again demonstrated the lack of agreement within the movement on whether it was appropriate to address the Israeli issue at the IAEA General Conference instead of the UN General Assembly or in the NPT context. The resolution had only four operative paragraphs, which called on Israel to join the NPT and place all its nuclear facilities under the IAEA safeguards, urged the director general to work on achieving this goal and requested that the Director General report accordingly to the GC.[84] The vote made a strong statement in advance of the 2010 NPT Review Conference that the Middle East issue would be central, and that the Arab states had NAM support on the issue. At the same time, it made the introduction of the INC Resolution at the 2010 GC inevitable, which was seen by many states and observers as detrimental to the preparations for the 2012 Middle East Conference.

As previously mentioned, the Middle East and INC were not normally seen as NAM issues at the IAEA. It was understood that NAM sympathised with the cause, but non-Arab states (except Iran) rarely played an active role. In 2007, however, the Cuban chair of the NAM Vienna Chapter for the first time sent a letter to the president of the General Conference in support of the Arab Group's request to re-introduce the 'Israeli Nuclear Capabilities and Threat' in the conference agenda. The Cuban representative was also exceptionally active in the conference floor debates and spoke forcefully, on behalf of NAM and in a national capacity, in support of the INC resolution and Arab amendments to the Middle East resolutions. It appears that after the failure to get a vote on the INC in 2006, the Arab Group in Vienna sought to draw on NAM support to shore up its votes. This approach was probably also affected by the close relationship between the Arab and Cuban delegations, and the prominent role played by the Iranian representative in the Vienna Chapter.

The case of the role of the NAM chair in Vienna and the NAM chair in New York during Cuba's tenure as chair of the Non-Aligned Movement underscores the important part that personalities play in shaping policy. In New York, Cuba often has been a moderating influence among the NAM hardliners; in Vienna, it has tended to be the standard bearer of the ideological struggle between the developing countries and the global North.

The character and dynamics of the NAM Chapter in Vienna are also influenced by the very active engagement of several particularly vocal NAM members, including Algeria, Venezuela and Iran, at the IAEA with respect to the INC and Middle East issues. Due to their influence, the Egyptian mission in Vienna in 2009 might have been constrained in its ability to maneuver and find a compromise with the West. It is not surprising, therefore, that in 2010, when the conflict over the INC resolution again became intense, a compromise proposal emanated from the Coordinating Bureau in New York rather than from the NAM Chapter in Vienna.

Failure to compromise (again): 2010

As discussed in the preceding chapter, the 2010 NPT Review Conference resulted in the adoption of a consensus action plan, one of the main elements of which was a set of recommendations on the Middle East. For the first time, a consensus decision mandated that institutional arrangements be put in place to begin implementation of the 1995 Resolution on the Middle East. It was agreed that the UN secretary-general and the three co-sponsors of the 1995 resolution (Russia, the UK and the United States), in consultation with states in the region, would convene a Middle East Conference in 2012 and, prior to that, would appoint a facilitator to conduct consultations for the organisations of the conference. The final document of the 2010 Rev Con also reiterated the call on Israel to accede to the NPT as a non-nuclear-weapon state.

Based on the Rev Con recommendations and the intensive negotiations that led to them, key policymakers in the United States and among its European allies appear to have concluded that they had demonstrated sufficient commitment to the Middle East NWFZ progress. They therefore believed that it was unnecessary and imprudent for the Arab states to again introduce an INC draft that had the potential to undermine the progress that had recently been made related to the Middle East. The Arab states, or at least their representatives in Vienna did not, however, share this perspective, possibly due to the disparaging remarks that Israel made immediately after the Rev Con, which appeared to signal that it was not prepared to participate in the 2012 Conference.

The resolution on Israeli Nuclear Capabilities adopted in 2009 mandated the IAEA director general to consult with member states and report on implementation of the resolution. Aware that there had been limited response to the director general's letter on the matter, the Arab states raised the implementation question at the June 2010 meeting of the Board of Governors. This move, which was met with consternation at the Board, signalled that notwithstanding the outcome of the 2010 Rev Con, the Arab states were unlikely to drop the INC issue at the upcoming General Conference. It probably also spurred both the United States and the EU to mount an early campaign to defeat the INC resolution in September 2010.

A US envoy visited Vienna in August 2010 in an unsuccessful effort to persuade the Arab Group not to table an INC draft. Accounts of precisely what transpired are vague and inconsistent. As best one can discern from interviews, it appears that the US official asked the Arab states to withdraw the item 'Israeli Nuclear Capabilities' from the agenda altogether or simply to refrain from tabling a draft resolution. In either case, it is unclear if anything was offered in return, such as a statement by the conference president and support for a consensus on the Middle East resolution, as was done before 2006. It may well be that the United States believed that it had spent enough political capital in May to obtain consensus at the Review Conference by naming Israel in the Final Document, and that there was no need to make additional offers to secure goodwill from the Arab states on the INC issue. Some accounts also suggest that the US representative made it very clear to the Arab states that the prospects for the 2012 Middle East Conference would be derailed in the event that the resolution was introduced. In addition, a linkage was likely made to the Arab–Israeli peace process, as the Obama administration had invested considerable effort in pushing for the resumption of talks and the extension of the settlements construction freeze that was due to run out at the end of September 2010.

In the intervening period between the conclusion of the Rev Con and the 2010 General Conference, Israel sent mixed messages about the 2012 conference, and some US officials believed that its participation was not inconceivable. No progress, however, had been made on appointing the facilitator or selecting a venue for the conference as mandated by the Rev Con. Buoyed perhaps by their victory in 2009, but also convinced that compromises in past years had not brought progress, the Arab states pressed on for a vote on the INC resolution. This time, however, the United States, having invested early in lobbying member states (and particularly smaller NAM countries in Africa), succeeded in defeating the resolution when it came up for a vote in the General Conference.

No bridge builders emerged from the NAM Vienna Chapter or any other political groupings at the IAEA. However, shortly before the start of the conference, a proposed compromise from a NAM state arrived from New York. Never introduced officially on the conference floor, the so-called 'Philippines proposal' entailed the adoption of two items in lieu of the vote on the INC. One was a decision/resolution postponing the consideration of the INC to the next session of the General Conference and a request for the director general to report that session on the implementation of the 2009 resolution. The second was a proposed resolution requesting that the IAEA provide assistance (for example, by conducting studies and consultations) in organising the 2012 Middle East Conference. For procedural reasons, the two resolutions/decisions had to be introduced before the agenda item on the INC, which required the agreement of the sponsors of the INC Resolution. The Arab states agreed and asked the NAM to mandate the Philippine ambassador in Vienna to negotiate on behalf of the NAM Chapter with the EU and other Western states regarding the compromise proposal. Ironically, it was three non-Arab NAM members – Iran, Cuba and Venezuela – that had the most difficulty with the proposed compromise, as well as with authorising the Philippine representative to speak on behalf of the movement. Egypt insisted, however, that the Philippine ambassador be given full support. The participation of the Philippines was obviously linked to the fact that the 2010 Rev Con was chaired by one of its most senior ambassadors, Libran Cabactulan, and the proposed compromise was presented as a way to preserve the achievement of the Rev Con on the Middle East issue.

Western states did not raise any specific concerns about the text of the compromise proposals but postponed giving a definitive response. They also expressed doubts about NAM unity and the readiness of the movement to support the proposals even if the West blessed them, apparently alluding to Iran and Venezuela. The waiting game ended on the penultimate day of the conference when the United States and the EU indicated they would not support the Philippine proposal. No attempt was made to use procedural means to block the INC resolution from being considered, and ultimately it was defeated by a vote of 46 in favour, 51 against, and 23 abstentions.[85] Of those who voted for the resolution in 2009, Burkina Faso, Ghana, Mongolia, Niger, Singapore and Thailand abstained in 2010, and Serbia was absent from the room. All the additions to the votes against and in favour were from states that had not participated in the vote in 2009. Two additional abstentions (Lesotho and Mauritius) came from states that did not vote in 2009, either. It is also noteworthy that a number of Latin

American countries, including Brazil, Chile, Mexico and Peru, abstained on the Israeli Nuclear Capabilities resolution in both 2009 and 2010, and none of them spoke in explanation of the vote. Indicative of the length to which the United States and its allies went to defeat the INC was the appearance at the vote of a number of states that rarely attend the General Conference. According to one participant from a large NAM delegation that often made use of the seats allocated to a much smaller adjacent state, a delegate appeared just in time for the vote, asked him to please move from her delegation's seat, cast a negative vote and departed, never to return.[86]

After the vote, the US ambassador sounded upbeat, suggesting that the defeat of the resolution somehow allowed the states to 'set aside the divisiveness' of past debates and placed them 'in a stronger position to pursue the noble goal of a Middle East free of weapons of mass destruction'.[87] Interestingly, in explaining their votes, the representatives of both Singapore and Thailand referred not to the 2010 NPT Rev Con decision, but to the Palestinian–Israeli peace talks, which suggests that the United States used that issue rather than the NPT to convince delegations not to support the resolution.[88]

The INC resolution may have produced no clear winners, but it resulted in a lot of bad blood that threatened to continue poisoning the atmosphere in Vienna. Developments at the 2011 General Conference, however, offered a partial reprieve from the acrimony. Questioning in early summer 2011 the US commitment to implementing the 2010 Rev Con recommendations on the Middle East, the Arab states again requested to inscribe the INC item on the General Conference agenda. At the same time, they delayed the circulation of a draft INC resolution to their NAM colleagues, which indicated uncertainty about the following course of action.[89] The question of what would happen with the INC and its implications for the 2012 conference was one of the main sources of concern and tension ahead of the GC session in 2011. After intensive internal consultations and just four days before the start of the General Conference, the Arab group decided not to table a draft resolution. The reasons behind this decision were the progress achieved by mid-September in narrowing down the options for a facilitator and the host country for the 2012 Middle East conference, and the Arab states' concern that submitting a draft resolution would be used by the United States and Israel as an excuse to discontinue engagement on the matter.[90] As the INC-centred tension was eliminated, the parties were able to finally reach an agreement and choose, in October 2011, Jaakko Laajava of Finland as the facilitator.

Active involvement of the non-aligned states in the promotion of the INC resolution tested the limits of NAM solidarity and added one more highly divisive issue to the menu of NAM–West interactions in Vienna. Along with the discussion of Iran's and Syria's compliance with their respective safeguards agreements, the INC debate and process revealed the high degree to which deliberations at the IAEA have become politicised, pitting the Western states and the Vienna Chapter of NAM against each other. One implication of this trend is its potential effect on the NPT review process. The first meeting of the Preparatory Committee for the 2015 NPT Review Conference is scheduled to take place in Vienna in spring 2012, and the new and unfortunate 'spirit of Vienna' may well affect NPT proceedings there.

NAM and nuclear security/nuclear terrorism

As noted earlier, traditionally nuclear security has not been a NAM issue in the context of the IAEA. Instead, it has been treated as a technical rather than political subject that is most appropriately addressed by the G-77 as part of its mandate on

IAEA activities related to 'nuclear safety and security'. Most NAM members appear to prefer that the issue be discussed as a technical matter, but in recent years the subject has become increasingly politicised. As a result of this shift, various items related to nuclear security have become the focus of debate in Vienna, including UN Security Council Resolution 1887 and the Washington Nuclear Security Summit.

The historical context

Historically, the issue of nuclear security has meant different things to different parties. In fact, in a number of languages there is little if any distinction between 'safety' and 'security', and even experienced interpreters confuse the words.[91] The distinction turns on the matter of intent: security pertains to the intentional use of nuclear material for malicious purposes while safety refers to unintended consequences such as reactor malfunction.

Adding to this lack of conceptual clarity has been the significant change in orientation by those involved in safeguarding nuclear material from an initial focus on states as potential proliferators (and the need to detect and prevent the diversion of nuclear materials from peaceful uses into clandestine national weapons programmes) to the subsequent recognition of the danger that non-state actors might engage in a variety of acts of nuclear terrorism.[92] The NPT, negotiated in the 1960s, has no provisions that address the risks posed by non-state actors, and although the IAEA began to engage on nuclear security issues in the early 1970s, its focus was state-centric.[93] Even the surge of interest in the dangers of illicit nuclear trafficking and 'loose nukes' following the collapse of the Soviet Union was initially conceived mainly in terms of the need for enhanced physical protection, material control, and accounting to guard against nuclear material falling into the hands of would-be state proliferators. More broadly, the international non-proliferation regime at the turn of the century had few mechanisms in place to deal with nuclear terrorism challenges.

Only after the horrific events of 11 September 2001 did the international community and the IAEA refocus their attention on the previously under-appreciated dangers posed by non-state actors. In 2002 the IAEA created the Office of Nuclear Security under the Department of Nuclear Safety and Security, and in March 2002 its Board of Governors approved 'in principle' an ambitious action plan 'designed to upgrade worldwide protection against acts of terrorism involving nuclear and other radioactive materials'.[94] Subsequent revelations about the international nuclear supply network associated with A.Q. Khan reinforced senior IAEA officials' inclinations to emphasise the urgency of the threat and the need for a coordinated international response.[95] Since then, the agency has undertaken a wide range of activities to promote nuclear security and protect against nuclear terrorism, including steps devoted to information collection and assessment, provision of advisory services, education and training, and emergency preparedness.[96]

NAM as a group has never addressed the issue of nuclear security or nuclear terrorism at the Board of Governors or the General Conference, although the G-77 has spoken on several occasions with respect to the agency's Nuclear Security Plan.[97] The NAM ministerial meeting in Bali in May 2011 made no reference to nuclear security, and prior ministerial and summit documents provide little guidance to NAM chapters about the appropriate positions to follow. To the extent that the subject is addressed, commentary is typically confined to support for 'an appropriate international regime for physical protection of radioactive materials during their transportation',[98] the welcoming of action in multilateral forums such as the UN General Assembly to prevent terrorists from acquiring weapons of mass destruction,[99] and implicit criticism of similar action by the less representative UN Security Council.[100] Notwithstanding the absence of a well-developed formal NAM stance – or, perhaps, in part due to it – the reactions of non-aligned countries to the new and expanded activities of the IAEA in the sphere of nuclear security and terrorism have not been uniform. They have varied considerably depending on the nature of specific initiatives.

Despite this variation, there exist a number of common elements in NAM perspectives. They include:

1. a view that the basic source of nuclear insecurity and terrorism is the continued possession of nuclear weapons by a small number of states;

2. concern that a new focus on nuclear security may divert the agency from its core competencies and deplete funding for technical cooperation or the agency's other promotional functions;[101]

3. apprehension that undue attention to the security of nuclear material and facilities will diminish international cooperation on peaceful uses and inflate the cost of nuclear power generation; and

4. the belief that any additional activities undertaken by the agency with regard to protecting against nuclear terrorism should be funded by voluntary, extra-budgetary contributions.

Although not a consensus view, many NAM members and observers also appear to attach a higher priority to securing radioactive sources than to securing fissile material, due to the fact that radioactive material can be found in large quantities in a number of developing countries, though very few possess highly-enriched uranium (HEU) or plutonium.[102]

The Vienna Chapter of NAM was not directly engaged in the debate during or subsequent to the negotiation in 2004 of

UN Security Council Resolution 1540, which required all states to implement measures aimed at preventing non-state actors from acquiring weapons of mass destruction, related materials and their means of delivery. This lack of active involvement was to be expected as the issue was a UN matter for which the NAM Coordinating Bureau had primary responsibility. One might have assumed that the same situation would obtain in September 2009 when the UN Security Council adopted Resolution 1887, a measure that addressed a number of nuclear disarmament, non-proliferation and terrorism issues. In fact, however, the NAM Vienna Chapter took the lead in criticising the resolution for its failure to take NAM positions into account in the formulation of the document (despite the fact that a number of NAM members and observers were members of the Security Council at the time) and with respect to several points in the resolution that related to the work of the IAEA.[103] In particular the Vienna Chapter objected to what it described as the resolution's attempt 'to reverse the order of priorities of the agency by giving primacy to safeguards and safety considerations in a manner that leads to the restriction of the promotional role of the agency' and to set new conditions and prerequisites for nuclear exports. It also objected to the resolution's failure to recognise 'the need for a comprehensive multilaterally negotiated instrument prohibiting attacks or threat of attack on nuclear facilities devoted to peaceful uses of nuclear energy'. Noticeable by its absence from the Chapter's statement, however, was any reference to language in the resolution that supported the need to enhance security to prevent terrorists from acquiring weapons-useable nuclear material, to convene a Nuclear Security Summit in 2010, to lock down all vulnerable nuclear-weapons material within four years (a goal proposed by President Obama), to share best practices as a practical way to strengthen nuclear security, and to minimise the use of HEU in the civilian nuclear sector 'to the greatest extent that is technically and economically feasible'.[104] Had the letter from the Vienna Chapter only been sent to the IAEA director general, it probably would have gone relatively unnoticed. By sending the same letter to UN secretary-general Ban Ki-moon, however, the Vienna Chapter provoked a dispute within NAM over the appropriate jurisdiction of its different chapters and the disproportionate influence within the movement of some members.[105]

The strange case of HEU minimisation

A diverse and increasing number of countries now recognise the terrorist risks associated with the civilian use, storage and trade in HEU. However, the modest language on the subject adopted in UN Security Resolution 1887, and similar text subsequently endorsed by the 2010 Nuclear Security Summit in Washington and the 2010 NPT Final Document, represents a major shift in position for several key NAM states, including most importantly South Africa, Egypt, Malaysia and Algeria. Although NAM has never taken a formal position on HEU minimisation, until very recently, these states – led by South Africa – were inclined to oppose initiatives that sought to combat nuclear terrorism by eliminating or minimising the use of and commerce in HEU for civilian purposes. At least one of these countries also sought – successfully – to discourage the IAEA from adding HEU minimisation to its expanding list of nuclear security initiatives.

Space does not allow for a full accounting of this long and convoluted tale.[106] The most important elements of the story, however, illustrate the significant influence that nuclear knowledge confers on a small number of countries in intra-NAM deliberations and interactions with non-NAM members, the opportunity such know-how affords to cloak national policy objectives in the guise of NAM interests, the significant role personalities play in shaping policy and the potential for major policy change on the part of NAM members, notwithstanding the aforementioned factors.

More specifically, in the initial aftermath of the 2005 NPT Review Conference, where HEU minimisation was first raised in the NPT context and met with little opposition, senior officials at the IAEA and in the US government had high expectations that international consensus in support of the principle of HEU elimination, or at least minimisation, in the civilian sector could soon be achieved. This view was shared by IAEA Director General Mohamed ElBaradei, who at the 2005 Rev Con had spoken in favour of the elimination of HEU in peaceful nuclear applications. Several countries, led by the United States and Norway, also believed they could obtain support for a resolution on the subject at the autumn 2005 IAEA General Conference. Although this ambition proved unrealistic – in part because of inadequate preparations, as well as a very heavy-handed US approach – most supporters of HEU minimisation remained optimistic about the prospects for a consensus resolution the following year. This optimism, however, largely evaporated after South Africa voiced major reservations about the HEU initiative during a two-part International Symposium on Minimization of HEU in the Civilian Nuclear Sector in Oslo in June 2006, hosted by the Norwegian government in cooperation with the IAEA.

Although the technical portion of the symposium, which attracted experts from more than 40 countries, produced consensus that conversion from HEU to low-enriched uranium was possible in most instances and that current conversion programmes have been largely successful, the more policy-oriented portion of the symposium failed to produce agreement on a clear path forward. Most participants acknowledged that HEU minimisation was a desirable objective, but views diverged about the relative emphasis that should be given to civilian and military programmes. Opinions also varied on the wisdom of linking an initiative to reduce HEU in the civilian nuclear sector to broader non-proliferation and disarmament goals. The spokesperson for South Africa, in particular, argued that 'WMD terrorism should not be pretext for removing rights', and that efforts to promote HEU minimisation could undermine the 'inalienable right' of NPT states parties to peaceful nuclear use. Moreover, the South African diplomat asserted that an emphasis on HEU minimisation in the civilian nuclear sector had the effect of 'disarming the disarmed'. Although these charges are not well founded[107] and probably reflect the fact that South Africa possesses the only significant HEU stocks in the Non-Aligned Movement, the South African argument resonated among several of the other NAM representatives present and undermined what had previously been perceived by most observers to be a non-discriminatory initiative.[108]

As a result of the stance taken by South Africa at the Oslo Symposium, the general ignorance by most other NAM delegations about the technical issues associated with reactor conversion, the high esteem with which South Africa was held within NAM, and the close personal relationship between the South African representative on the IAEA Board of Governors and the IAEA director general (as well as with key officials in the Norwegian foreign ministry), both the leadership of the IAEA and the Norwegian government soon decided to adopt a much more cautious stance toward HEU minimisation at the IAEA and in the NPT review process. The IAEA director general dropped his public support for the initiative, the agency chose to take no note of the consensus document that had emerged from the technical portion of the Oslo Symposium, and Norway shifted its strategy to one in which greater emphasis was placed on voluntary measures that did not require consensus. This reorientation occurred despite the fact that NAM never formally discussed the issue of HEU minimisation or took a position on the subject as a collective. Indeed, with the notable exception of South Africa, which had a significant commercial interest in the use of its HEU reserve for the production of medical isotopes, few NAM members had any interest in the topic, as it was not seen as having a direct impact on their national security interests.

This situation might well have continued indefinitely had the United States not chosen to include HEU minimisation as one of the planks it promoted in UN Security Council Resolution 1887.[109] None of the six NAM members and observers on the Security Council at the time appears to have opposed the language, although it is unclear how much attention they paid to the issue. Support for the measure by China, which previously had not expressed its views on the subject, also may have made it easier for the non-aligned states to accept. More surprising was the omission of any reference to HEU minimisation in the letter from the Egyptian Chairman of NAM to the IAEA director general (and copied to the UN secretary-general), which was very critical of other elements in the Security Council resolution.

Whatever the explanation for NAM (and South African) silence on the subject in the context of the Security Council action, the issue was again raised directly during the extended negotiation of the Communiqué and Work Plan of the 2010 Nuclear Security Summit. Given this background, the role played by representatives of South Africa, Egypt, Algeria and Malaysia in the negotiation of these documents was especially remarkable.[110] Although the language adopted on HEU minimisation was not as strong as the United States would have preferred, it basically echoed what had been agreed upon in the much smaller UN Security Council forum, and was endorsed by the heads of state or government of 47 countries, including a number of key NAM members.[111] Reportedly, this endorsement did not come easily for several NAM states (or several close allies of the United States), whose foreign ministries and ministries of science and education were divided on the wisdom of reducing reliance on HEU. Ultimately, however, they decided that the political gesture in support of the Obama administration's initiative was more important than any economic or other justification for opposing HEU minimisation. This outcome from a large but still 'extra-multilateral' negotiating forum was embedded more fully in a traditional multinational framework when nearly identical language was adopted on HEU minimisation at the 2010 NPT Review Conference. As noted in Chapter Two, there was surprisingly strong support for the initiative at the NPT Rev Con by several NAM observers, while the main resistance came from two of the closest allies of the United States.

It does not appear that the NAM Vienna Chapter ever specifically discussed the issue of HEU minimisation in the context of the Nuclear Security Summit. A number of NAM countries not invited to the Washington meeting, however, did seek to mobilise NAM for the purpose of criticising the forthcoming summit. These snubbed members of the movement may have had reservations about the substantive focus of the summit, but their primary objection was the exclusive nature of the event. While these critics succeeded in convening a plenary meeting of NAM to discuss the summit, no consensus decision was reached, and Egypt and other NAM members invited to the summit indicated that they would attend in their national capacity. Interestingly, subsequent to the April 2010 meeting, a number of originally sceptical NAM participants have become much greater enthusiasts for the process.[112]

NAM and the emerging nuclear safety–security nexus

Historically, nuclear security/terrorism has been viewed by most developing countries as a technical issue insofar as it relates to the IAEA, albeit one with political undertones. The G-77 rather than NAM therefore has chosen to speak on the subject with reference to the agency's nuclear security programme, and for the purpose of making the case that it is an extra-statutory activity that requires voluntary, extra-budgetary funds. However, in light of several recent developments, it is quite possible that in the near future NAM will also become directly engaged on nuclear security matters. This almost certainly will be the case if the Nuclear Security Summit process continues, and if efforts are made to reference the summit outcomes in General Conference resolutions. The issue also is apt to acquire a more political dimension in the aftermath of the Fukushima nuclear accident and through the growing sentiment at the IAEA and elsewhere that one cannot readily separate nuclear safety and security activities. The 2012 Seoul Nuclear Security Summit thus will include a new focus on the safety–security nexus, as did the High Level Meeting on Nuclear Safety and Security at the United Nations on 22 September 2011. The safety–security nexus might also have implications for the current NPT review cycle: speaking at the High Level Meeting, UN Secretary-General Ban Ki-moon already called on the NPT member states to allocate specific time for the discussion of nuclear safety and security at the Prep Com meeting in spring 2012.[113] The NAM statement at the New York event proved difficult to negotiate and reflected the competing interests and expertise of the NAM Coordinating Bureau in New York and the Vienna Chapter. Although the negotiated document did not focus on very specific nuclear security matters such as HEU minimisation, it would not be surprising in the future for NAM to express an expanded and updated position on the nuclear safety–security nexus, a subject of growing concern to both NAM and non-NAM states.

Conclusions

Diplomats and observers bemoan the politicisation and polarisation at the IAEA, and the damaging effect of this trend on the agency's ability to carry out its mandate. From the vantage point of many NAM members, the United States and other Western countries are largely responsible for this circumstance through their efforts to limit the developing countries' access to peaceful nuclear uses while exploiting non-proliferation-related issues for political purposes. Western diplomats and policymakers, for their part, believe the NAM has acted irresponsibly by abusing the right to peaceful uses, resisting necessary non-proliferation measures, and introducing extraneous issues, such as Israeli nuclear capabilities, into the IAEA agenda. They also fault NAM for not lending more support when a response is needed to non-compliance or lack of cooperation by one of its own members. In fact, as the examples in this chapter illustrate, both sides have contributed to the polarisation at the agency in recent years, at times due to short-sighted policies founded on a poor understanding of and lack of respect for each other's interests and motives.

Although some of the points of contention are new, others have festered for a long time. As Lawrence Scheinman points out in his 1987 book about the IAEA, politicisation was a serious problem for the agency then in relation to growing disagreements between the North and the G-77 about the voluntary nature of contributions to the Technical Cooperation Fund.[114] Furthermore, in 1982 – following the Israeli attack on the Osiraq reactor, near Baghdad – a vote at the General Conference rejecting the credentials of the Israeli delegation led the United States and 14 other delegations to withdraw from the conference. At that time, the United States threatened to 'halt general participation in agency activities, including payments of its contributions'.[115] In other words, although we may fondly recall the 'spirit of Vienna', times have been both better and worse.

The establishment of the NAM Vienna Chapter in 2003 coincided with the rise in tensions between the United States and NAM (and much of the rest of the world as well), and both reflected the broader state of international relations and increased the political dimension of the debate at the IAEA.

The push to adopt a resolution on Iran in September 2005, and the resulting vote, gave rise to a pattern of non-consensus decision-making at the Board of Governors that has contributed to a very contentious political climate. Subsequently, votes were taken on resolutions dealing with Iran's nuclear programme, proposals for assurance of supply, and implementation of safeguards in Syria. At the General Conference, increased confrontation and greater resort to voting were precipitated in part by the (re)introduction of the Israeli Nuclear Capabilities agenda item and draft resolution. Since 2006, votes also were taken on the resolution on safeguards in the Middle East, the EU-sponsored resolution on implementation of safeguards and the Model Additional Protocol, as well as the nuclear security/terrorism resolution.

On the one hand, the tendency now for board members to vote more readily may have the salutary effect of depriving individual states of a virtual veto power, and could facilitate a move away from 'business as usual,' which often has meant doing nothing. An inclination to abandon consensus decision-making in favor of voting, however, also reduces incentives to search for common ground and diminishes the states' ownership of the board's decisions and actions. One approach is not necessarily better than the other in all instances, but policymakers need to reflect on the trade-offs between adopting decisions quickly and securing the broadest possible support for the implementation of various initiatives.

A striking finding in this chapter is the diminished ability of NAM to capitalise on its overall numerical advantage at the IAEA when it comes to voting as a bloc. Although NAM has never enjoyed such an advantage on the Board of Governors, where it numbers less than half the total, one might have expected it to prevail on most votes in the General Conference. However, as illustrated by the votes on the Israeli Nuclear Capabilities Resolution, NAM struggles to maintain discipline as a political group when forced to vote. Votes cast by different NAM members often reflect their relations with the United States and EU, and associated economic, trade and political interests, as much or more than their collective NAM principles or national non-proliferation preferences. As a NAM diplomat explained to the authors, while statements of positions are formulated primarily by the representatives in Vienna, decisions on important votes are likely to be taken at a higher political level. This situation favours the more powerful states that have the ability to exert leverage in other capitals regardless of the views of those diplomats posted at the IAEA. This same phenomenon also works to NAM's disadvantage during votes on the board (for example, on Iran compliance), where it is even more difficult for NAM to muster a majority. Much to NAM's chagrin, in recent years the EU and 'associated' states have emerged as a more cohesive voting bloc, typically with a greater convergence of views. This phenomenon is partly due to the considerably smaller size of the EU and, more importantly, to the much greater cultural, economic and political homogeneity of its members. As discussed in Chapter One, the growing numbers and diversity of NAM members over the years have made it more difficult for the movement to formulate a common position when members are forced to choose between immediate pragmatic considerations and more abstract principles – a tension that voting at the IAEA highlights.

CHAPTER FOUR

Looking to the future

NAM celebrated its 50th anniversary in September 2011.[1] Not surprisingly, the world – and NAM – looks very different today than it did when the movement first convened in Belgrade, Yugoslavia, in 1961. The host country for the first summit no longer exists, the East–West bloc structure that gave rise to the establishment of NAM has long since disappeared, and the movement's membership has surged from 25 to 120 – an extraordinarily diverse group of countries that now includes both highly developed states and several nuclear-weapon possessors. Still, NAM has retained much of its original identity and sense of purpose as a champion of the security of its members, defender of the global South in its struggle for equality and social justice, and social movement to advance the economic and political interests of countries from the developing world.

A comparison of the 1961 Heads of State/Government Belgrade Declaration and the recent 2011 ministerial-level Bali Final Document (and the associated Bali Commemorative Declaration) reveal important elements of continuity and change in NAM perspectives and priorities. Particularly relevant to the focus of this book is the consistent identification of disarmament in both the 1961 and 2011 documents, and in other past summit declarations, as an imperative and urgent task. Although there is a greater sense of urgency in the earliest declaration about the need to reduce nuclear risks, as well as a more direct linkage to the potential for war between the two nuclear superpowers, it is notable that the very first item in the 21-item list of objectives to which NAM foreign ministers at the Bali meeting subscribed also deals with the need to promote nuclear disarmament, international security and stability.[2] Unlike the Belgrade Declaration, however, which does not mention peaceful nuclear use, the Bali Commemorative Declaration highlights, as part of the first item on disarmament, a concomitant obligation to ensure the inalienable right of all states to peaceful uses of nuclear energy. This obligation is reiterated in expanded form in the Final Document.[3] Unlike the 1961 declaration, the 2011 Final Document makes reference on several occasions to the issue of nuclear proliferation. It clearly specifies, however, that nuclear disarmament remains the highest priority, and stresses that efforts aimed at nuclear non-proliferation 'should be parallel to simultaneous efforts aiming at nuclear disarmament'.[4]

The neglect or subordination of nuclear non-proliferation in the aforementioned declarations typifies NAM's more general aversion to many of the non-proliferation initiatives promoted by the United States and its allies (and also frequently Russia), which NAM perceives as discriminatory restrictions on the inalienable right of developing countries to exploit nuclear energy for peaceful purposes. As Russell Leslie observes in one of the few scholarly analyses of differences between NAM and Western attitudes towards the NPT and non-proliferation, 'some NAM members believe that technology holders are not really interested in limiting proliferation and are instead primarily interested in limiting economic development in "southern states"'.[5] More generally, he notes correctly that Western states tend to attribute high intrinsic value to non-proliferation activities and regard them as 'valuable in their own right', while NAM is inclined to view them as but one element of the NPT bargain.[6]

NAM's disinclination to emphasise non-proliferation issues in its summit declarations (other than to call for Israeli membership in the NPT) can largely be explained by the low position that proliferation prevention occupies in NAM's hierarchy of goals. More perplexing is NAM's historical readiness to avoid internal debate and public commentary on core values involving nuclear disarmament when they conflict with the behaviour of the movement's own members. Indeed, among the greatest challenges for NAM in the past and present is determining how to maintain a credible voice and principled stance on nuclear disarmament directed at the five NPT-recognised nuclear-weapons states – the United States, Russia, the United Kingdom, France and China – while simultaneously appearing to gloss over the nuclear tests and expanding arsenals of three of its own members.[7]

This conundrum initially arose when India detonated its first nuclear explosion in 1974. The test represented a technological accomplishment that was regarded with pride by many NAM members, but also a development that was difficult to reconcile with the movement's principled opposition to nuclear arms. This cognitive dissonance was only partially reduced by New Delhi's less-than-convincing attempt to portray the explosion as a 'peaceful nuclear test'. The dissonance became much more pronounced in 1998, when India carried out more tests without any pretense of a peaceful motive, and when its South Asian NAM rival Pakistan quickly followed suit. The nuclear test by the DPRK in 2006 brought the number of NAM nuclear-weapons possessors to three, a critical mass that is hard to dismiss, especially given the rapid growth of nuclear arsenals and delivery vehicles in South Asia and the rise in regional tensions there and in Northeast Asia.

While NAM might prefer to ignore the internal inconsistencies in the application of its disarmament principles, it became more difficult to avoid the contradictions when the United States chose to reverse course on its own nuclear trade policy towards India in 2005.[8] Strains within NAM were aggravated further when the United States, Russia, France and the United Kingdom campaigned aggressively to modify export guidelines in an India-friendly fashion at the Nuclear Suppliers Group (NSG). NAM already had a history of complaints against the NSG, whose perceived cartel-like behaviour was considered inhospitable to the peaceful-use developmental needs of the movement's members. The fact that some NAM members and observers on the NSG – Brazil, Kazakhstan and South Africa – supported the special exemption for India placed them at loggerheads with the majority of NAM, including a very vocal group of Arab states and Iran, which were concerned that Israel could benefit from the NSG precedent.

This division within NAM remains very pronounced today, and is likely to persist for some time as the issue of NSG guidelines in general, and their applicability to India in particular, continues to dominate NSG deliberations.[9] Recent efforts by the United States to promote Indian membership in the Nuclear Suppliers Group also can be expected to generate additional debate and divisions both within the NSG and among NAM members and observers. Although it is difficult to assess how issue-specific this rift is for NAM, it would appear to be indicative of the growing pains of the movement, which now includes a number of economically prosperous states with major nuclear industries and export aspirations and capabilities. From the perspective of these more developed non-aligned states, it is reasonable for economically driven policy decisions that serve national interests to diverge at times from prevailing NAM preferences without signalling any diminished commitment to the fundamental norms and ideals of the movement. Such policy disagreements are, after all, normal in any large body or association.

There is little doubt that NAM can withstand occasional internal disputes such as that prompted by the NSG exemption to India and voting at the IAEA Board over the issue of Iranian compliance. Should these contentious cases multiply and defections from collective positions become more frequent, however, NAM's bargaining power vis-à-vis the West will be eroded, as will its identity, legitimacy and image as a guardian of shared values and goals. Under such circumstances, the traditional meaning of NAM consensus could be reduced to formal statements that bear little resemblance to the actual positions staked out by members.[10] In addition, one would have to question the extent to which NAM members themselves rely on the movement's negotiated positions and traditional core precepts as a basis for formulating their national positions on nuclear matters.

To be sure, the Non-Aligned Movement is not the only political grouping that prides itself on adherence to principled positions or occasionally finds it difficult to reconcile the conflicting pressures of remaining true to long-held collective values and making pragmatic compromises. More than most groupings, however, the movement has enshrined very clearly the principles to which its members formally subscribe, and it reiterates them on a regular basis at ministerial meetings and summits. This approach may be useful in promoting policy continuity and helping to coordinate a very large and diverse collective. It may have been valuable in the past in providing broad policy guidance to members on issues where many states lack national expertise, such as those in the nuclear sector. A major risk of this approach, however, is inertia and the potential for an increasing number of countries to question the relevance of long-standing collective positions to pressing current national needs.

Our study has discerned significant intra-NAM differences on a variety of nuclear issues both within the NPT review process and at negotiating forums in Vienna. In some instances, these divisions have presented opportunities for Western states and selected NAM members to collaborate in strengthening nuclear non-proliferation, peaceful use and anti-nuclear-terrorism initiatives in a fashion that would have been difficult to achieve had all NAM states adhered closely to past declarations and maintained tight group cohesion. In the NPT context, however, it was NAM's ability to act in concert that made possible the negotiation of a consensus final document. One must therefore be cautious not to assume that greater NAM disarray will necessarily be helpful in advancing Western policy objectives. The readiness of some NAM members to depart from the movement's formal positions in their pursuit of specific policy initiatives should also not be confused with a diminished appreciation by most NAM states of the value of the movement. Indeed, member states continue to be very proud of the movement's history, its increasing membership, and what they regard as its ongoing political relevance and impact in multilateral forums. For many of them, NAM not only affords their representatives a seat at negotiating tables that otherwise would be beyond reach, but also provides a protective barrier and a sense that 'one is not alone'.[11] Similarly, though there are numerous instances in which group solidarity has broken down, one should not underestimate the continuing power of the concept of solidarity, which in the NAM context means rhetorical and political support for members who suffer harm, whether of an economic, political or military nature.[12]

Competing tendencies within NAM to adhere to shared principles, promote collective policy goals and accommodate the public expression by member states of different national priorities has led to considerable tension and what one observer has called 'schizophrenic behaviour'.[13] This characterisation is apt, but is one that applies to most large and long-established organisations. What remains to be seen is the extent to which NAM can continue to serve as the guardian of the group's core values and goals, while simultaneously addressing the needs of its member states in an international environment that bears little resemblance to the era in which it was founded. This is a major challenge for the movement as a whole and for the next chair of NAM in particular.

NAM with Iran as chair

The tendency in the West to view NAM in un-nuanced terms and to gloss over intra-NAM politics contributes to a lack of general interest in or attentiveness to the possible impact on NAM policy of Iran's assumption of the chair of the movement in mid-2012. Although the implications of Iran's chairmanship are difficult to anticipate, and will undoubtedly be influenced by a number of domestic and international developments, some relevant information may be gleaned from an examination of the behaviour of prior NAM chairs, such as Cuba, which were reviled in the West for their ideological orientation and anti-American/anti-Western political agenda. Also possibly indicative of the approach that Iran will employ when it becomes NAM chair is its behaviour thus far as current chair of the G-77 in Vienna.

It is interesting to review international commentary about Cuba and NAM during the late 1970s, in advance of Cuba's assumption of the NAM chair for the first time. As A.W. Singham and Shirley Hune have observed, at that time '[t]here was great fear among conservative non-aligned countries that Cuba would radicalise the Movement and use illegitimate methods to propagate its own foreign policy'.[14] This concern, which the United States sought unsuccessfully to exploit, was evident from the time Cuba was selected as the forthcoming chair at the Colombo Heads of State/Government Summit in 1976 until the conclusion of the Havana Summit three years later. The internal debate took place mainly at Coordinating Bureau meetings at the United Nations in New York and in other venues, and at a Ministerial Meeting in Belgrade in 1978. For the most part, the debate focused on issues involving criteria for membership in the movement, the role of the socialist states within NAM, the concept of equidistance from the United States and the Soviet Union, as well as a re-examination of the appropriate meaning of 'consensus'. Although ostensibly different topics, they all were linked to questions about the normative meaning of NAM, its core identity, and the extent to which the movement should define itself in terms of shared principles or in opposition to some external parties or 'outside other'. These more philosophical questions were also grounded in the very immediate concern of states such as Singapore, Saudi Arabia, Egypt, and Yugoslavia, among others, that as NAM chair Cuba might attempt to exploit the absence of more formal decision-making rules to promote its own foreign-policy agenda – for example by arbitrarily finding a consensus consistent with national preferences when in fact none existed.[15] Singham and Hune report that some sceptics worried that Cuba might even transform the Coordinating Bureau into a 'Central Committee'.[16]

Some of these concerns were allayed at the bureau meeting in Havana in May 1978. At that time, voices within NAM already were advocating postponement of the next summit, which was scheduled for September 1979, or a change in venue. Although Cuba did not alter its views on controversial international matters (for example, its interventionist policy in Africa) in order to curry favour with more conservative NAM members at the meeting, it carefully separated its interventions as a delegation on the floor and its role as chair of the bureau meeting, where it appears to have acted in an impartial fashion.[17] Although efforts continued both within and outside of NAM to replace the summit chair designate – and even to expel Cuba from the movement – and despite very heated debate on these issues at a meeting of NAM foreign ministers in Belgrade in late July 1978, ultimately NAM closed ranks against what many saw as a Western effort to divide the movement. At the Belgrade meeting, only seven states from Africa and the Middle East chose to express reservations regarding the selection of Havana as the site for the next summit.[18] However, in an attempt to ensure that Cuba would not hijack the meeting, Havana was asked to circulate its draft of the summit declaration two months before the gathering, rather than immediately before as per the traditional practice.[19]

In some respects, the actual Havana Summit in 1979 was anticlimactic. All but two of the 95 members of NAM at the time attended, and although debates were often intense, major confrontations were avoided. For the most part Cuba was successful in demonstrating an ability to distinguish between its role as impartial host and chair and a forceful advocate for a national agenda that did not necessarily resonate with many NAM members. Perhaps most significantly, the Havana Summit demonstrated the capacity of the Non-Aligned Movement to withstand a major challenge to its integrity, to accommodate ideological diversity and to preserve collective solidarity on a set of core principles in the face of divergent national interests.[20]

Obviously, Fidel Castro's Cuba is not the same as Iran under Ayatollah Sayyid Ali Khamenei and Mahmoud Ahmadinejad. Their national (and personal) agendas, as best one can discern, reflect very different priorities, and their threat perceptions, although not dissimilar in terms of the perceived dangers posed by the United States, are filtered through very different ideological and experiential lenses. In addition, as discussed above, the Non-Aligned Movement in the twenty-first century has changed in significant respects since the peak of the Cold War. That said, it is striking how much more relaxed most NAM members – and other states – appear to be about Iran's chairmanship than was the case when Cuba was selected to be NAM chair.

The current quiescence of outside parties probably reflects a tendency to gauge NAM policy today primarily in terms of issues associated with the Middle East, to assess that policy as extreme and to fail to contemplate how the positions could harden further when Egypt hands the baton to Iran. The absence of much expertise or sustained attention in the West to NAM politics and policies reinforces this perspective. It also contributes to the tendency to view NAM as far more homogeneous than it is and to minimise the impact of leadership change. Success in achieving a consensus final document at the 2010 NPT Review Conference in 2010 and in beating back the Israeli Nuclear Capabilities Resolution at the 2010 IAEA General Conference (as well as recent successes in securing support from key NAM members for major nuclear-security and fuel-assurance initiatives) probably reinforces complacency on the part of the United States and its allies about their ability to pursue their nuclear non-proliferation policies without taking into account who is at the NAM helm.

One can discern a similar lack of anxiety about the forthcoming NAM chair among members, despite the fact that Iran is under UN Security Council sanctions. Unlike the period of disquiet within the movement following the Colombo Summit, most NAM states appear confident that Iran will not abuse its position to promote national preferences at odds with those of most other members. This attitude may be the product of a combination of greater confidence in NAM institutions and practices; the knowledge of the movement's track record in withstanding major challenges and adapting to new circumstances; a belief that ideological pluralism remains, on balance, an asset; and the conviction that any attempt by Tehran to misuse its position to promote national preferences could be aborted by member states. In addition to these positive explanations, however, one cannot dismiss the possibility that quiescence also may be a function of wishful thinking, a failure to appreciate Iran's willingness to exploit the chairmanship as a foreign-policy tool, and a growing lack of interest on the part of some NAM members in the movement altogether. As several NAM diplomats explained, the less central the movement is to their countries' priorities, the less effort they are prepared to invest in shaping NAM policy and the more complacent they are about the direction charted by NAM leadership.

Although the importance of the movement may have waned for a number of NAM members, there is little doubt that Iran regards NAM as a key element in its multilateral foreign policy. Indeed, given Iran's pursuit of the NAM chairmanship, one must assume that the Iranian leadership believes that being at the movement's helm for three years will provide Tehran with a number of potential benefits in its pursuit of a variety of domestic and international objectives. These are likely to include, but are not limited to, support for the paramount goal of regime survival, continued development of the country's nuclear programme in all its aspects, avoidance of a major military strike (although some domestic factions could conceivably regard a limited military attack as politically advantageous), securing recognition as a regional leader, undermining implementation of international sanctions, and increased domestic and international legitimacy.

It is unlikely that Iran expects to gain many direct or substantial benefits from NAM in the pursuit of some of these objectives, such as fending off threats to the regime's survival or gaining recognition as a regional leader. It is not unrealistic, however, to assume that Tehran believes its chairmanship could be of major assistance in countering Western efforts to isolate the country internationally – both politically and economically – as NAM states almost uniformly dislike sanctions and perceive them to be tools of the developed world. It also should be noted that the priority assigned by the regime to these different objectives probably has changed since Iran secured its position in the NAM troika in 2006, and is likely to continue to evolve depending on internal and external developments. In addition, the importance attached to different objectives undoubtedly varies to some degree across domestic political factions, which may differ on such core issues as the ultimate purpose of the nuclear programme and the political and economic costs of international autarky and isolation.

Chairmanship of NAM affords Iran a number of potential advantages. Although the leadership in Tehran is ideologically comfortable with a confrontational approach to the West, the regime is wary of being isolated (or portrayed as such) within the region, and among developing countries more generally. Membership in NAM – not to mention chairmanship of the movement – therefore affords Iran both increased legitimacy and allies that are of use internationally and domestically. As chair of NAM, Iran may believe it can pursue a more assertive foreign policy with fewer risks. This mindset could tempt Iran to be an 'activist' chair that seeks to utilise the position to promote national policies that may not correspond closely to the views of many NAM members.

Such activism is most likely to manifest itself with respect to nuclear issues, which have dominated Iran's foreign policy in recent years and of which many NAM members have little technical knowledge. It is plausible, for example, to expect that chairmanship of NAM will reinforce Iran's already well developed tendency to influence the movement's positions and rhetoric on all things nuclear. In addition, it would be surprising if Iran did not seek to use the degree of deference normally afforded the chair to increase the attention which NAM devotes to peaceful nuclear-use issues – especially Article IV rights – and to assert these rights at every opportunity. Having greater control over the NAM agenda and the drafting and negotiating process at ministerial and summit meetings, as well as at the IAEA and the United Nations, and in the NPT review process, Iran may choose to gain further and more explicit endorsement from the movement for its nuclear programme, including the right to develop a complete fuel cycle.[21] It also may seek stronger language condemning attempts to politicise and abuse the IAEA.[22]

The NAM chairmanship, however, also comes with major risks for Iran. As one experienced NAM diplomat has noted, it will subject the country to much greater scrutiny from other NAM states than would otherwise be the case, especially on issues related to the Middle East. According to this interpretation, most NAM members will be inclined to follow Iran's lead on nuclear disarmament issues and will give it some leeway on peaceful uses, but a number of states will be prepared to push back if Iran attempts to redirect the movement on matters involving security in the Middle East and non-proliferation compliance.[23] If this view is correct, the United States and its Western allies run a risk that if they are perceived as pursuing a confrontational or inflexible approach on disarmament matters, for example in the NPT context, it may prompt NAM to close ranks around the Iranian chair and provide it with greater freedom to manoeuvre on other issues.

In attempting to gauge how much leeway Iran will have as NAM chair, one should keep in mind that not all chairs are equal and that much depends on the reputation and diplomatic prowess of the country in question, as well as the resources it has at its disposal. In this regard, while Iran has long had an exceptionally able diplomatic corps, in recent years it has purged some of its most talented diplomats, presumably for their ideological leanings. While Iran has more material and human resources at its disposal than many NAM members, it does not command the same level of broad support and respect within the movement as countries such as Egypt, Indonesia and South Africa. Not being a party to any regional structure, it also cannot rely on a cohesive support group such as, for example, the League of Arab States. As a consequence, while Iran probably can rely on help on most issues from a small number of NAM allies such as Cuba, Venezuela and Syria (depending on the future of the Bashar al-Assad regime), support from these states will not be sufficient to shape the movement's positions and pronouncements without buy-in from the traditional NAM leadership. One, therefore, should not exaggerate Iran's ability to manipulate the silent majority, especially in the event that leading NAM members such as Egypt, South Africa and Indonesia decide that Tehran has overstepped its role as NAM chair.

Further complicating Iran's ability to utilise NAM in promoting its own foreign policy is its eroding legitimacy among developing nations. This development is not only related to growing scepticism among a number of NAM states about its nuclear intentions, but stems from the regime's harsh response to domestic protests after the 2009 presidential elections and the country's irrelevance to much of the Arab world during and subsequent to the Arab Spring. In this regard, it would appear that the more Arab pride is restored by domestic change, the less Iranian defiance of the West resonates on the street. This is not to say that Iran no longer enjoys the sympathy of many members of NAM, especially on matters that pertain to perceived inequities involving socio-economic developmental issues such as peaceful nuclear use, or that Iran will not find new means to bolster its credentials among developing countries. It may decide, for example, to use its position as chair to champion efforts by Palestine to expand its presence in international forums – an issue on which there is little NAM dissent. Iran also may be able to generate broad support on a variety of nuclear-disarmament issues that are relatively uncontroversial within NAM. Nevertheless, miscalculation in this respect and overplaying the chairmanship card in a way that is perceived as elevating national objectives above those of greatest priority to the movement carries the risk of greater isolation for Iran.

Although extremely difficult to gauge (much less predict), domestic politics has the potential to greatly influence the course of Iranian foreign policy, including the manner in which Tehran attempts to use the chairmanship of NAM. Domestic political and bureaucratic battles, for example, have raised the value attached to conservative ideological credentials and appear to have become increasingly important criteria for promotion in both the nuclear- and foreign-policy establishments.[24] Domestic politics have indeed already affected Iran's engagement on the nuclear issue. For example, the failure to secure the low-enriched uranium (LEU) fuel-swap deal in late 2009–early 2010 was in large part due to internal disagreements and challenges to the authority of President Ahmadinejad.[25] Should this trend continue, one may expect greater departure from pragmatism in Iranian foreign policy and the pursuit by Iran of more ideologically driven positions. Under such circumstances, Iran might adopt a less cautious approach toward NAM and seek more blatantly to harness the movement for its own national purposes – an approach that might provoke serious resistance and prove counterproductive.

An intriguing preview of Iran's approach to chairmanship of NAM can be found in its performance to date as chair of the Group of 77 in Vienna. Although by mid-2011 it had only occupied that post for a relatively short period of time, its stewardship to date suggests that it may attempt to test how far it can go in imposing its own preferences before having to yield to determined opposition. For example, shortly after assuming the lead position in the G-77, the Iranian chair acted in a manner that a number of other key members regarded to be at odds with customary procedure. When a senior diplomat from a friendly state was appointed to an important position without adequate prior consultation among other G-77 members, an unusual series of complaints about abuse of process was raised by states as diverse as Singapore, India, Egypt, South Africa and Argentina.[26] In another instance more directly related to non-proliferation, the chair was able to persuade a sufficient number of G-77 members to adopt a position on the subject of safeguards confidentiality, after Iran had failed to get support on the same pet issue from NAM. As a result of this manoeuvre, the G-77 spoke to the IAEA Board in March 2011 on a topic it had never before addressed and that previously had been regarded as NAM's responsibility.[27] It remains to be seen how much of this behaviour can be explained in terms of the personality of the Iranian chair, the extent to which such behaviour will be repeated in light of the negative reaction it produced, and the readiness of NAM members to respond forcefully to similar instances of real or perceived arbitrary action on issues that generally involve lower stakes than the bread-and-butter economic and developmental matters that define the G-77.

Iran's role in shaping NAM policy on issues related to the NPT and the IAEA will also be significantly influenced by the progress (or lack thereof) regarding implementation of the 2010 NPT Final Document, especially the recommendations related to the Middle East. The selection in autumn 2011 of a facilitator and venue for the 2012 Middle East Conference has been welcomed by most of the key parties, including the current chair of NAM, although some states would have preferred more expeditious action.[28] This modest forward movement could create a relatively positive atmosphere at the 2012 NPT Prep Com, which will be held in Vienna in April–May 2012, during which time Egypt will still retain the position as NAM chair. At least in the short term, therefore, it is likely that Egypt and most other Arab states will encourage NAM as a collective to continue to support the bargain reflected in the 2010 NPT Final Document rather than reopening debates about disarmament that were papered over at the last Review Conference. NAM frustration over disarmament and peaceful-use issues, however, can be expected to rise significantly at the 2013 NPT Prep Com if 2012 passes without the convening of the Middle East Conference and without visible progress on the implementation of the Action Plan adopted by consensus in 2010.[29]

CONCLUSION

It is crucially important to engage NAM more constructively in tackling a variety of pressing nuclear disarmament, proliferation, peaceful-use and terrorism challenges. Productive collaboration with NAM on each of these fronts requires a more sophisticated understanding of NAM, and its shared core values and priorities, mode of decision-making, diversity and latent (and sometimes pronounced) tension among members and observers. This refers mainly to the tension between strict adherence to principled collective positions and pursuit of pragmatic national policies that may at times deviate from the NAM consensus. Regrettably, the un-nuanced views of many Western observers about the workings of NAM have their mirror image in many simplistic NAM perspectives on Western policymaking. In both instances, there tends to be a disregard for the role of personalities, domestic politics and bureaucratic interests in shaping foreign policy and an inclination for leaders from both NAM and the West to be most attentive to those in the other grouping with the loudest voices.

Some Western analysts have characterised the Non-Aligned Movement as a very large and increasingly dysfunctional family. While this analogy is not without merit, it tends to discount the powerful attraction that most NAM members feel towards a set of long-standing shared core values and principles, few of which are directly related to nuclear disarmament and non-proliferation. Many of these shared norms derive directly from the Bandung Conference and the first NAM summit in Belgrade and reflect the still powerful role that NAM plays as a defender of developing countries from the South. Western interlocutors must appreciate the continuing force of principles such as social justice, respect for national sovereignty and territorial integrity, and non-interference in internal affairs, since it is these principles that underpin the construct by which NAM members define their own identity and interpret Western initiatives in the nuclear sphere. In some areas, such as promotion of nuclear use for peaceful developmental purposes and support for multilateral disarmament machinery and greater adherence to international treaties, NAM and the West may discover that they have compatible objectives and ready avenues for forging common policy initiatives. The West needs to devote greater efforts to recognising these convergent interests where they exist and building upon them.

In other domains, such as enhanced nuclear safeguards and export controls, the overlap in NAM and Western priorities will be less obvious. Nevertheless, it is important to probe beyond the appearance of NAM uninterest and intransigence. Western negotiators may find that the differences between their positions and NAM's are less pronounced once they have distinguished among the movement's most vocal NAM members, the negotiated collective stance, and the national positions of many other members who may attach different values to non-proliferation measures based on individual calculations of national economic, political and security interests.[1]

It is particularly important for Western policymakers who wish to engage NAM more productively to distinguish between more extreme, anti-Western members and the often silent majority of the non-aligned. Countries that fall into the latter category may be reluctant to challenge NAM leaders and more hardline members on most nuclear-related matters, but they are not necessarily ill-disposed to tougher non-proliferation measures if they are non-discriminatory in nature and have the potential to address their own needs and national priorities.

NAM's receptivity to Western initiatives on non-proliferation, peaceful use and nuclear terrorism will be greatly enhanced if the United States (and other NWS) demonstrates through its actions, in addition to rhetoric, that it is serious about nuclear disarmament. The United States under President Obama has moved forward in this regard, albeit cautiously, and several of the other nuclear-weapons states also have taken modest steps in this direction. As noted in Chapter Two, these initiatives contributed to a positive atmosphere at the 2010 NPT Review Conference that in turn was conducive to the negotiation of a consensus Final Document. That said, most NAM members remain sceptical of the nuclear-weapons states' readiness to implement significant disarmament measures in the near term and are likely to insist on more concrete actions before they demonstrate a corresponding flexibility in their embrace of new non-proliferation commitments.

An important subgroup of Arab states within NAM will be even more insistent on a tit-for-tat approach when it comes to their adherence to a number of non-proliferation measures sought by the West. Although not uniform in their position, Egypt and a number of other Arab NAM states will, at a minimum, link their support for measures such as the Additional Protocol and the Comprehensive Test-Ban

Treaty to making headway in implementing the 1995 Middle East Resolution. By the same token, failure to implement the much more modest 2010 NPT Rev Con recommendations on the Middle East will almost certainly stymie any prospects for enlisting Egypt – and many other states from the region and elsewhere – in new non-proliferation initiatives.

Two decades ago, the collapse of the Soviet Union and disappearance of the Eastern Bloc compelled NAM to re-examine its *raison d'être*. The United Nations and the parties to the NPT have yet to undertake a similar serious review of practices adopted during the Cold War that have little relevance to the international political landscape in 2012. As a result, regional groupings persist in which Hungary, Poland and the Czech Republic, among other former Warsaw Pact countries, vie for administrative positions within the UN and the NPT review process reserved for the Eastern Bloc at the same time that they may hold leadership positions within the EU. This anachronistic process, while dysfunctional at times, also highlights the possibility for states to participate in new bodies that cut across old political boundaries and empower their pursuit of national interests without necessarily abandoning their ties to older institutions. The emergence of nuclear security as a major global issue and the creation of a host of new multilateral initiatives (including some not linked directly to the United Nations) has enabled many NAM states to craft mutually beneficial working relationships with Western countries even though these initiatives may not have the formal blessing of the Non-Aligned Movement. Illustrative of this development is growing acceptance within NAM for implementation of UN Security Council Resolution 1540 on preventing WMD terrorism, increased support for the Proliferation Security Initiative among NAM members (notwithstanding its association with President George W. Bush), and extensive representation by NAM members at the 2010 Nuclear Security Summit in Washington.[2] All of these initiatives were at one time or another regarded with great suspicion by most NAM members, but over time their value has been increasingly recognised.

Past disarmament and non-proliferation accomplishments in the NPT review process by the New Agenda Coalition – an unusual coalition of NAM and Western non-nuclear-weapons states – also demonstrate the potential for such hybrid groupings to engage in nuclear disarmament and non-proliferation bridge-building, as well as highlighting the current shortage of such associations. The articulate promotion by several European NNWS of a number of forward-looking disarmament items (including a nuclear-weapons convention) suggests the possible viability of a new nuclear disarmament coalition involving countries such as Switzerland, Ireland, Austria and Norway and a set of NAM counterparts. Even more broadly based coalitions involving one or more NWS may be possible, although the experience of the Norwegian-led Seven-Nation Initiative on Nuclear Disarmament and Non-proliferation is not encouraging in this regard.[3] A new ten-member grouping, the Non-proliferation and Disarmament Initiative (formerly the 'Friends of the NPT') has a smattering of NAM members and observers, but its ability to bridge the gulf between NWS and NNWS is inhibited by the disproportionately heavy representation of US allies.[4]

This study has noted the recurrent tendency for a relatively small number of states to dominate discussion of and decision-making on nuclear issues, while a much larger body of members defers to these opinion leaders. The authors' interviews with many senior and more junior NAM diplomats indicate that this phenomenon results from both the active pursuit of leadership positions by a small number of states and the lack of capacity of most countries for staking out informed, independent positions on what are complex, technical nuclear issues. This state of affairs is amenable to change, but that is unlikely to occur unless far more disarmament and non-proliferation training opportunities are provided to NAM members who currently lack institutional and personnel capacity in these spheres. In the past the government of Norway has supported small training programmes designed to remedy this shortfall, but a much greater investment is needed in this sector.[5]

Engaging with NAM should entail greater empathy and improved understanding of the movement's interests and perceptions. By the same token, NAM members would profit from avoiding old and simplistic caricatures of the West, unfortunately often reinforced by some hardline US media commentators, many of whom do not accurately reflect US or Western policy motivations and goals. Engagement also means having more informal consultations with NAM counterparts throughout the process of developing proposals and policies that would affect them – instead of presenting new rules and initiatives without careful consideration of potential reactions, selling them to the easily convinced, criticising those with strong dissenting opinions, and trying to push the decisions through smaller bodies that are easier to navigate. Finding compromise solutions is not easy and by necessity does not yield the most desired outcome, but it allows for a greater buy-in and ownership of initiatives and, as a consequence, greater commitment to implementation. The more inclusive approach will not convert all die-hard opponents, especially considering that the positions of the most hardline states are greatly affected by the generally confrontational relationship with the West, far beyond the nuclear sphere. It will, however, have the virtue of reducing the space for these states to engage in ideological posturing, manipulation of debate, and exploitation of existing grievances among the developing countries.

Achieving a broad-based agreement takes longer than passing a Security Council resolution or launching an initiative by a few like-minded states. However, in searching for solutions, it is desirable for both Western states and NAM members to heed an African proverb: If you want to go fast, walk alone; if you want to go far, walk together.

List of members, NAM and the G-77

Table 2. **Non-Aligned Movement, Group of 77**

COUNTRY	NAM	G-77
Key: ◆ = member / O = observer		
Afghanistan	◆	◆
Algeria	◆	◆
Angola	◆	◆
Antigua and Barbuda	◆	◆
Argentina	O	◆
Armenia	O	
Azerbaijan	◆	
Bahamas	◆	◆
Bahrain	◆	◆
Bangladesh	◆	◆
Barbados	◆	◆
Belarus	◆	
Belize	◆	◆
Benin	◆	◆
Bhutan	◆	◆
Bolivia	◆	◆
Bosnia and Herzegovina	O	◆
Botswana	◆	◆
Brazil	O	◆
Brunei Darussalam	◆	◆
Burkina Faso	◆	◆
Burundi	◆	◆
Cambodia	◆	◆
Cameroon	◆	◆
Cape Verde	◆	◆
Central African Republic	◆	◆

COUNTRY	NAM	G-77
Chad	◆	◆
Chile	◆	◆
China	O	◆
Colombia	◆	◆
Comoros	◆	◆
Congo (Republic of the)	◆	◆
Congo (Democratic Republic of the)	◆	◆
Costa Rica	O	◆
Côte d'Ivoire	◆	◆
Croatia	O	
Cuba	◆	◆
Djibouti	◆	◆
Dominica	◆	◆
Dominican Republic	◆	◆
Ecuador	◆	◆
Egypt	◆	◆
El Salvador	O	◆
Equatorial Guinea	◆	◆
Eritrea	◆	◆
Ethiopia	◆	◆
Fiji	◆	◆
Gabon	◆	◆
Gambia	◆	◆
Ghana	◆	◆
Grenada	◆	◆
Guatemala	◆	◆
Guinea	◆	◆
Guinea-Bissau	◆	◆
Guyana	◆	◆
Haiti	◆	◆
Honduras	◆	◆
India	◆	
Indonesia	◆	◆
Iran (Islamic Republic of)	◆	◆
Iraq	◆	◆
Jamaica	◆	◆
Jordan	◆	◆
Kazakhstan	O	
Kenya	◆	◆
Korea (Democratic People's Republic of)	◆	◆
Kuwait	◆	◆
Kyrgyzstan	O	
Laos (People's Democratic Republic)	◆	◆
Lebanon	◆	◆
Lesotho	◆	◆
Liberia	◆	◆
Libya	◆	◆

COUNTRY	NAM	G-77
Madagascar	◆	◆
Malawi	◆	◆
Malaysia	◆	◆
Maldives	◆	◆
Mali	◆	◆
Marshall Islands		◆
Mauritania	◆	◆
Mauritius	◆	◆
Mexico	O	
Micronesia (Federated States of)		◆
Mongolia	◆	◆
Montenegro	O	
Morocco	◆	◆
Mozambique	◆	◆
Myanmar	◆	◆
Namibia	◆	◆
Nepal	◆	◆
Nicaragua	◆	◆
Niger	◆	◆
Nigeria	◆	◆
Oman	◆	◆
Pakistan	◆	◆
Palestine	◆	◆
Panama	◆	◆
Papua New Guinea	◆	◆
Paraguay	O	◆
Peru	◆	◆
Philippines	◆	◆
Qatar	◆	◆
Rwanda	◆	◆
Saint Kitts and Nevis	◆	◆
Saint Lucia	◆	◆
Saint Vincent and the Grenadines	◆	◆
Samoa		◆
São Tomé and Principe	◆	◆
Saudi Arabia	◆	◆
Senegal	◆	◆
Serbia	O	
Seychelles	◆	◆
Sierra Leone	◆	◆
Singapore	◆	◆
Solomon Islands		◆
Somalia	◆	◆
South Africa	◆	◆
Sri Lanka	◆	◆
Sudan	◆	◆
Suriname	◆	◆

COUNTRY	NAM	G-77
Swaziland	◆	◆
Syrian Arab Republic	◆	◆
Tajikistan	O	◆
Thailand	◆	◆
Timor-Leste	◆	◆
Togo	◆	◆
Tonga		◆
Trinidad and Tobago	◆	◆
Tunisia	◆	◆
Turkmenistan	◆	◆
Uganda	◆	◆
Ukraine	O	
United Arab Emirates	◆	◆
Tanzania	◆	◆
Uruguay	O	◆
Uzbekistan	◆	
Vanuatu	◆	◆
Venezuela	◆	◆
Vietnam	◆	◆
Yemen	◆	◆
Zambia	◆	◆
Zimbabwe	◆	◆
Membership totals:	120	131
	(Obs – 17)	

Prior Non–Aligned Movement heads of state or government summits

Table 3. **Prior Non–Aligned Movement heads of state or government summits**

	Date	Location
1st summit	1–6 September 1961	Belgrade, Yugoslavia
2nd summit	5–10 October 1964	Cairo, Egypt
3rd summit	8–10 September 1970	Lusaka, Zambia
4th summit	5–9 September 1973	Algiers, Algeria
5th summit	16–19 August 1976	Colombo, Sri Lanka
6th summit	3–9 September 1979	Havana, Cuba
7th summit	7–11 March 1983	New Delhi, India
8th summit	1–6 September 1986	Harare, Zimbabwe
9th summit	4–7 September 1989	Belgrade, Yugoslavia
10th summit	1–6 September 1992	Jakarta, Indonesia
11th summit	14–20 October 1995	Cartagena de Indias, Colombia
12th summit	29 August–3 September 1998	Durban, South Africa
13th summit	20–25 February 2003	Kuala Lumpur, Malaysia
14th summit	11–16 September 2006	Havana, Cuba
15th summit	11–16 July 2009	Sharm el-Sheikh, Egypt

NOTES

Introduction

[1] It is exceeded in size only by the Group of 77 (G-77), which has grown from its original founding complement of 77 in 1964 to 131 members. The G-77 constitutes a loose coalition of nations focused on issues of economic development.

[2] A very recent and significant exception is the paper by former Singapore diplomat Yvonne Yew, 'Diplomacy and Nuclear Non-Proliferation: Navigating the Non-Aligned Movement', Discussion Paper no. 2011-07, Harvard Kennedy School, 13 June 2011. See also Russell Leslie, 'The Good Faith Assumption: Different Paradigmatic Approaches to Non-proliferation Issues', *Non-proliferation Review*, vol. 15, no. 3, November 2008, pp. 479–97. Very few of the more general works on NAM pay more than passing attention to nuclear issues. See, for example, Peter Willetts, *The Non-Aligned Movement: The Origins of a Third World Alliance* (London: Frances Pinter Ltd., 1978); M.S. Rajan, V.S. Mani and C.S.R. Murthy (eds), *The Nonaligned and the United Nations* (New York: Ocean Publications, Inc., 1987);

and A.W. Singham and Shirley Hune, *Non-Alignment in An Age of Alignments* (Westport, CT: Lawrence Hill & Co., 1986).

[3] This research was supported by Carnegie Corporation of New York, the Hewlett Foundation, the Norwegian Ministry of Foreign Affairs, and the British Foreign and Commonwealth Office.

[4] The 137 NAM members and observers represent more than 72% of the membership of the NPT, which numbers 189 states parties.

[5] 'NAM consensus', however, does not imply unanimity; rather, it presupposes that 'sufficient agreement' exists among member states.

[6] Some members reportedly even suggested that NAM focus exclusively on economics and merge with the G-77, while others proposed that the movement's name was anachronistic and should be changed. For commentary on the shift in emphasis see Cedric Grant, 'Equity in International Relations: A Third World Perspective', *International Affairs*, vol. 71, no. 3, July 1995, p. 568; and Ednan

Agaev and Sergei Krylov, 'Non-Aligned Movement: 116 Nations', *International Affairs*, vol. 52, no. 3, 2006, pp. 48–9.

7   See 'Working Paper Submitted by the Members of the Group of Non-Aligned States Parties to the Treaty on the Non Proliferation of Nuclear Weapons', 2010 NPT Review Conference, New York, 28 April 2010, available at http://www.un.org/ga/search/view_doc.asp?symbol=NPT/CONF.2010/WP.46; and 'Elements for a Plan of Action for the Elimination of Nuclear Weapons', Working paper submitted by the Group of the Non-Aligned States Parties to the 2010 NPT Review Conference, New York, 28 April 2010, available at http://www.un.org/ga/search/view_doc.asp?symbol=NPT/CONF.2010/WP.47.

8   For a brief discussion of prior IAEA General Conference debates over this resolution, see Leslie, 'The Good Faith Assumption', p. 488.

9   Interviews in Washington, DC with senior US government officials in the months prior to the 2010 IAEA General Conference.

Chapter One

1   Brioni, Yugoslavia, was the site of an informal meeting among Josip Broz Tito, Jawaharlal Nehru and Gamel Abdel Nasser in July 1956.

2   Lyrics from 'Song of the Non-Aligned', quoted in Akhil Gupta, 'The Song of the Nonaligned World: Transnational Identities and the Reinscription of Space in Late Capitalism', *Cultural Anthropology*, vol. 7, no. 1, February 1992, p. 64.

3   Some analysts are sceptical of the degree to which NAM was ever truly non-aligned and point to its tendency to adhere more closely to the political positions of the Soviet-led Eastern Bloc. As one NAM diplomat put it in an off-the-record interview with one of the authors in April 2011, 'non-alignment during the Cold War was really alignment in disguise'. Moreover, as one former diplomat from Sierra Leone has perceptively observed, NAM was not overly enthusiastic on those rare issues in the UN system where the Cold War rivals tended to collaborate, such as nuclear non-proliferation. See Davidson Nicol, 'The Major Powers in the United Nations and the Nonaligned Group', in M.S. Rajan, V.S. Mani and C.S.R. Murthy (eds), *The Nonaligned and the United Nations* (New York: Oceana Publications, Inc., 1987), p. 167. Another pointed but not totally off-the-mark observation regarding the nature of non-alignment during the Cold War, reportedly made by Sri Lankan President J.R. Jayewardene shortly after assuming office, was that there were only two non-aligned countries in the world: the Soviet Union and the United States. See Signham and Hune, *Non-Alignment in an Age of Alignments*, p. 54.

4   See the website of the 15th Summit of the Non-Aligned Movement, http://www.nameegypt.org/en/AboutName/HistoryAndEvolution/Pages/default.aspx#ten.

5   The entire list of objectives appears in Part 12 of the Declaration. See

'Nonaligned Countries Declaration, 1979 (Havana Declaration)', in Osmańcyzk, *Encyclopedia of the United Nations and International Agreements*, third edition, vol. 3 (New York: Routledge, 2003), pp. 1,600–1.

6   Interviews in Monterey, California in April 2011 by the authors with a former NAM diplomat; Osmańcyzk, *Encyclopedia of the United Nations and International Agreements*, p. 1,621.

7   Ednan Agaev and Sergei Krylov, 'Non-Aligned Movement: 116 Nations', *International Affairs*, vol. 52, no. 3, 2006, pp. 48–9.

8   'Nonaligned Countries Declaration, 1989 (Belgrade Declaration)', in Osmańcyzk, *Encyclopedia of the United Nations and International Agreements*, pp. 1,615–6.

9   According to the Cartagena Document of Methodology, which was adopted at the NAM Ministerial Meeting in Cartagena de Indias, Columbia, in May 1996, the category of NAM observer was introduced to 'promote the opening of the Movement to the contributions of other actors in the international arena'. NAM observers must meet the same criteria for admission as members, which include solidarity with the movement and adherence to and respect for the principles and objectives of NAM. These criteria are detailed in the Cartagena Document on Methodology, which appears as Annex 1 in the official document of the 14th Summit Conference of Heads of State and Government of the Non-Aligned Movement, Havana, Cuba, 11–16 September 2006, available at the website for the 15th Summit of the Non-Aligned Movement, Sharm el-Sheikh, http://www.namegypt.org/ en/relevantdocuments/pages/default. aspx.

10   See, for example, http://www. namegypt.org/en/relevantdocuments/ pages/default.aspx.

11   Singham and Hune, *Non-Alignment in an Age of Alignments*, p. 33.

12   See Annex 1: Cartagena Document on Methodology, as referenced in 'The Methodology of the Non-Aligned Movement'.

13   One of the authors has participated in several of these meetings, which were characterised by wide-ranging and often probing discussions that reflected a greater diversity of views than often exhibited at professional meetings of American political scientists and International Relations scholars.

14   For an analysis of Resolution 1887, see Keegan McGrath and Vasileios Savvidis, 'UNSC Resolution 1887: Packaging Non-proliferation and Disarmament at the United Nations', Nuclear Threat Initiative Issue Brief, 22 December 2009, http://www.nti.org/e_ research/e3_unsc.html.

15   For an overview of the orientation of NAM's Vienna Chapter, see Yvonne Yew, 'Diplomacy and Nuclear Non-Proliferation: Navigating the Non-Aligned Movement', Discussion Paper no. 2011-07, Harvard Kennedy School, 13 June 2011.

16   Even some senior NAM diplomats who were interviewed for this study were unaware of the movement's activities outside of New York and Vienna.

17   For an analysis of South Africa's role at the NPT Review and Extension Conference see Jayantha Dhanapala and Randy Rydell, *Multilateral Diplomacy and the NPT: An Insider's Account* (Geneva: United Nations,

2005); and Tariq Rauf and Rebecca Johnson, 'After the NPT's Indefinite Extension: The Future of the Global Non-proliferation Regime', *Non-proliferation Review*, vol. 3, no. 1, Fall 1995, pp. 28–44.

18 The Cartagena Document on Methodology stipulates that, while the observers can attend and address NAM Summits, they are barred from participating in the committees, working groups and task forces. In reality, the rule does not seem to be enforced, as several observers, such as Brazil and Mexico, are active participants, at least in the Disarmament Working Group.

19 In 1990, at the initiative of Egypt, the concept of a Middle East NWFZ was expanded to include all weapons of mass destruction. This more comprehensive approach envisaged the possibility that a bargain could be struck in which Israel agreed to abandon its unacknowledged but widely assumed nuclear-weapons capability while all other states in the region agreed to give up or forgo any chemical- and biological-weapons capabilities. See Patricia Lewis and William C. Potter, 'The Long Journey Toward a WMD-Free Middle East', *Arms Control Today*, vol. 41, no. 7, September 2011, pp. 8–14.

20 Interview with NAM diplomat by the authors, April 2011 in Monterey, California.

21 See Yew, 'Diplomacy and Nuclear Non-Proliferation: Navigating the Non-Aligned Movement', pp. 9–10.

22 *Ibid.*, pp. 6–9.

23 For a discussion of NAM through the prism of transnational identities, see Gupta, 'The Song of the Nonaligned World', pp. 63–79.

Chapter Two

1 NAM membership expanded most recently in May 2011, when Azerbaijan and Fiji were admitted as members, so the actual membership at the time of the 2010 NPT Review Conference was 118, with 115 parties to the NPT. The latter number excludes North Korea, whose NPT status was never officially settled after the announced withdrawal in 2003.

2 The legal status of the membership of the Democratic Republic of Korea, which declared its withdrawal from the Treaty in 2003, remains in dispute. The number cited excludes the DPRK.

3 Among its operative paragraphs, the 1995 Resolution on the Middle East 'endorses the aims and objectives of the Middle East Peace process ... calls upon all states in the region that have yet to do so, without exception, to accede to the Treaty as soon as possible and to place their nuclear facilities under the full scope of the International Atomic Energy Agency safeguards; Calls upon all States of the Middle East that have not yet done so, without exception, to take practical steps in appropriate forums aimed at making progress toward, inter alia, the establishment of an effectively verifiable Middle East zone free of weapons of mass destruction...; [and calls upon all States party to the NPT],

and in particular the nuclear weapon States, to extend their cooperation and to exert their utmost efforts with a view to ensuring the early establishment by regional parities to a Middle East zone free of nuclear and all other weapons of mass destruction and their delivery systems'. The resolution was co-sponsored by the three NPT depositary states (Russia, the United Kingdom and the United States) and adopted by the 1995 NPT Review and Extension Conference by consensus. 'Resolution on the Middle East', NPT/CONF.1995/32 (Part I), Annex.

4   See 'Working Paper Submitted by the Non-Aligned States Party to the NPT', NPT/Conf.2010/WP.46, 2010 Review Conference of Parties to the NPT, 28 April 2010; and 'Elements for a Plan of Action for the Elimination of Nuclear Weapons', working paper submitted by the Non-Aligned States Parties to the NPT, NPT/Conf.2010/WP.47, 2010 Review Conference of Parties to the NPT, 28 April 2010.

5   Summary Record, 8th Review Conference of the States Party to the Treaty on the Non-Proliferation of Nuclear Weapons, 3–28 May 2010, NPT/CONF.2010/50, vol. III, p. 161–2.

6   *Ibid.* pp. 165–8. Overall, the atmosphere in the hall was that of subdued relief (and slight confusion) rather than joy at having adopted a Final Document.

7   Mohamed I. Shaker, *The Nuclear Non-Proliferation Treaty: Origin and Implementation, 1959–1979*, vol. I (London/Paris/New York: Oceana Publications, Inc., 1980), pp. 37–8.

8   *Ibid.* Due to its neutrality, Sweden associated itself with the non-aligned states serving on the Eighteen-Nation Disarmament Committee, while

Brazil and Mexico were, and remain, influential observer states.

9   Quoted in Shaker, *The Nuclear Non-Proliferation Treaty: Origins and Implementation*, p. 37. While the predominant view among Western policymakers and diplomats today seems to be that loop-holes are contained in Article IV (peaceful uses) and Article X (withdrawal), the primary concern reflected in principle (a) was nuclear sharing, or the transfer of nuclear weapons from one state to another as part of a military alliance, a clear allusion to NATO.

10   *Ibid.* pp. 46–9. While Shaker is correct to emphasise how NAM and other states' support for the main elements of the NPT was crucial in its development, the main parts of the treaty were the product of direct negotiations between the United States and the Soviet Union.

11   For example, the NAM Working Paper on Disarmament tabled at the 2010 Review Conference demanded complete nuclear disarmament by 2025. See NPT/Conf.2010/WP.47.

12   See Shaker, *The Nuclear Non-Proliferation Treaty*, pp. 55–6, 59–60; and William Epstein and Paul C. Szasz, 'Extension of the Nuclear Non-Proliferation Treaty: A Means of Strengthening the Treaty', *Virginia Journal of International Law*, vol. 33, no. 4, Summer 1993.

13   Shaker, *The Nuclear Non-Proliferation Treaty*, pp. 80–2.

14   When the final text of the Treaty was presented to the UN General Assembly for endorsement in May 1968, attached to Resolution 2373 (XXII), Brazil and India abstained on the resolution. India, dissatisfied with the discriminatory nature of the treaty and insufficient commitment to

disarmament, famously called the new regime a 'nuclear apartheid'.

15 Shaker, *The Nuclear Non-Proliferation Treaty*, pp. 81–3.

16 For an in-depth, detailed and fascinating account of the 1995 Review and Extension Conference, see Rebecca Johnson, 'Indefinite Extension of the Non-Proliferation Treaty: Risks and Reckonings', *The Acronym Institute*, Report No. 7, September 1995, http://www.acronym.org.uk/acrorep/a07ext.htm.

17 David A.V. Fischer and Tariq Rauf, 'The Politics of the 1995 Conference on the Review and Extension of the Nuclear Non-Proliferation Treaty', uunpublished manuscript, CNS, 1995.

18 NAM's involvement in these negotiations merits a much more detailed discussion, but is beyond the focus of this chapter.

19 Johnson, 'Indefinite Extension of the Non-Proliferation Treaty: Risks and Reckonings'.

20 Comments from a NAM diplomat involved in the negotiations at the 1995 Review and Extension Conference, summer 2011.

21 Notably, the 'objectives' were added to principles at the insistence of Indonesia, who wanted to include a set of specific disarmament objectives in both the Extension and Review parts of conference documents. See Johnson, 'Indefinite Extension of the Non-Proliferation Treaty: Risks and Reckonings'.

22 Final Document, 7th Review Conference of the States Parties to the Treaty on the Non-Proliferation of Nuclear Weapons, NPT/CONF.2000/28 (Vol. I).

23 Slovenia was an original member of the NAC, but left the coalition shortly after its formation.

24 See Johnson, 'The Indefinite Extension of the Non-Proliferation Treaty: Risks and Reckonings'; and Fischer and Rauf, 'The Politics of the 1995 Conference on the Review and Extension of the Nuclear Non-Proliferation Treaty'.

25 Conversation with a 2000 NPT Review Conference delegate, spring 2011.

26 Brazil and Mexico, while active in NAM deliberations, are observers rather than members.

27 For a discussion of this trend see, for example, William Potter, 'India and the New Look of US Non-proliferation Policy', *The Nonproliferation Review*, vol. 12, no. 2, July 2005, pp. 343–54. See also Sverre Lodgaard, *Nuclear Disarmament and Non-Proliferation: Towards a Nuclear-Weapon-Free World?* (New York and London: Routledge, 2010). In fairness to the United States, Washington was not alone in its neglect of NPT commitments, and many NWS and NNWS – including leading members of NAM – engaged in selective inattention when economic opportunities clashed with non-proliferation obligations. As is discussed below, nowhere was this cherry-picking of obligations more apparent than with respect to nuclear trade with India.

28 Slowness in response was not confined to NAM, and many non-NAM states, including those in the developing world, have been missing in action.

29 See, for example, M.S. Rajan (ed.), *Nonalignment and the Nonaligned Movement in the Present World Order* (Delhi: Konark Publishers, 1994).

30 Cedric Grant, 'Equity in International Relations: A Third World Perspective', *International Affairs*, vol. 71, no. 3, July 1995, p. 568. See also Rajan, *Nonalignment and the Nonaligned Movement in the Present World Order*,

especially the chapters 'Nonalignment in the "Unipolar" World' and 'Nonalignment in the Post-Cold War Era'. The nuclear tests by India and Pakistan in 1998 also presented NAM with another major dilemma: how to remain an effective and principled advocate for nuclear disarmament while two of its members were building nuclear arsenals.

31 For an analysis of the 2009 NPT Prep Com, see Miles Pomper, 'Report from the NPT Preparatory Committee 2009', James Martin Center for Nonproliferation Studies, Washington DC, 26 May 2009, http://cns.miis.edu/stories/090526_npt_report.htm.

32 *Ibid.*

33 The remarks were made at a small gathering devoted to a discussion of prospects for bridging the NWS–NNWS/NAM divide in the run-up to the 2010 Review Conference. Meeting in Geneva attended by one of the authors in spring 2009.

34 See Keegan McGrath and Vasileios Savvidis, 'UNSC Resolution 1887: Unpacking the Resolution's Political Significance and Implications for the International Non-proliferation Regime', Issue Brief, *Nuclear Threat Initiative*, 3 February 2010, http://www.nti.org/e_research/e3_unsc_1887_part_2.html. Interviews conducted by one of the authors indicate that NAM requested but was denied the opportunity to address the Security Council Summit. NAM then forwarded its positions on nuclear disarmament and non-proliferation, abstracted from the Sharm el-Sheikh summit document, as a letter to the Security Council for consideration in its deliberations. The product of those negotiations, UNSCR 1887, was viewed as unsatisfactory by NAM even though a number of NAM members and observers sat on the Security Council. Interviews with NAM diplomats, New York, autumn 2009.

35 The recommendations on disarmament, for example, included expression of concern about security doctrines of the nuclear-weapons states, including nuclear sharing under NATO, reaffirmation of the importance of transparency, verifiability and irreversibility in nuclear-disarmament measures, the need for negotiating a fissile-material treaty on the basis of the Shannon Mandate, etc. Recommendations on safeguards and verification, inter alia, reaffirmed the role of the IAEA as 'the sole competent authority [in] verifying and assuring compliance' with safeguards agreements, emphasised the distinction between legal obligations and voluntary confidence-building measures, and rejected the politicisation of the IAEA work. There were 14 recommendations for the text on peaceful uses of nuclear energy, including the reaffirmation of states' rights and the need to respect their choices in peaceful uses, concern over 'undue restrictions on exports to developing countries' of technology and materials, and the necessity for caution in examining the issue of assurances of fuel supply.

36 See William Potter, Patricia Lewis, Gaukhar Mukhatzhanova and Miles Pomper, 'The 2010 NPT Review Conference: Deconstructing Consensus', James Martin Center for Nonproliferation Studies, Monterey, CA, 17 June 2010, http://cns.miis.edu/stories/pdfs/100617_npt_2010_summary.pdf.

37 On one occasion, NAM amendments were so numerous that the diplomat

who had to read them all out practically lost his voice by the end of the paper.

38 Conversation with a conference participant, autumn 2010.

39 As discussed in Chapter One, one must distinguish between the formal principle of non-hierarchical decision-making by consensus in which each state has an equal vote, and the actual process by which a relatively small number of very active NAM states prepare NAM positions, which are then endorsed at ministerial and summit meetings. The operation of the non-hierarchical principle tends to be more evident in large meetings and with respect to issues that the more influential members regard as less consequential.

40 'NAM Position as of 18 May 2010' on the NPT/Conf.2010/MC.II/CRP.1, Paragraph 14.

41 See, for example, 'Resolutions and Decisions adopted by the General Assembly during its 10th Special Session', A/S-10/4, United Nations, 23 May–30 June 1978, paragraph 60; as well as the Final Document of the Sharm-el-Sheikh Summit of Heads of State or Government. The motivation for Syria's action was clearly to circumvent the need for Israel's concurrence as one of the states in the region.

42 Conversations with conference participants who were engaged in these negotiations, summer 2010 and spring 2011.

43 The president of the first NPT Review Conference in 1975 was an ambassador from Sweden, a country that associated itself with the non-aligned at the Eighteen-Nation Disarmament Committee but was never formally a NAM member or observer. Presidents

of the Review Conferences between 1980 and 2010 came from Iraq, Egypt, Peru, Sri Lanka, Brazil and the Philippines.

44 See Potter et. al., 'The 2010 NPT Review Conference: Deconstructing Consensus', pp. 6–7.

45 Contained in NPT/CONF.2010/WP.47.

46 Conversations with NAM diplomats and comments from a member of the International Commission on Nuclear Non-proliferation and Disarmament, spring/summer 2011.

47 Even diplomats who were highly supportive of disarmament and ambitious measures noted, in private, that the approach presented in the paper weakened the movement's negotiating position.

48 States that persistently referred to the 2025 end-date were Cuba and Iran.

49 Dr. R.M. Marty Natalegawa, Foreign Minister of the Republic of Indonesia, 'Statement on Behalf of the NAM States Party to the Treaty on the Non-Proliferation of Nuclear Weapons before the 2010 Review Conference', New York, 3 May 2010, available at http://www.un.org/en/conf/npt/2010/statements/statements.shtml.

50 Final Document of the 2010 NPT Review Conference, Conclusions and Recommendations, paragraph B.iii, NPT/CONF.2010/50.

51 For complete statements and summaries, see the website of Reaching Critical Will at http://www.reachingcriticalwill.org/legal/npt/nptindex1.html.

52 Michele Calmy-Ray, Foreign Minister of Switzerland, 'Statement before the 2010 Review Conference of the Treaty on the Non-Proliferation of Nuclear Weapons' (in French), New York, 3 May 2010, available at http://www.un.org/en/conf/npt/2010/statements/

statements.shtml. See also Ken Berry, Patricia Lewis, Benoît Pélopidas, Nikolai Sokov and Ward Wilson, 'Delegitimizing Nuclear Weapons: Examining the Validity of Nuclear Deterrence', James Martin Center for Nonproliferation Studies (with support from the Swiss Federation), Monterey, CA, May 2010, http://cns.miis.edu/opapers/pdfs/delegitimizing_nuclear_weapons_may_2010.pdf.

53 Final Document of the 2010 NPT Review Conference, Conclusions and Recommendations, paragraph A.v, NPT/CONF.2010/50.

54 Conversation with a NAM diplomat, New Yok, autumn 2011. Among other things, India does not support the NAM push for the Fourth Special Session on Disarmament (SSOD IV) of the UN General Assembly.

55 Costa Rica, a NAM observer state that tabled a draft Nuclear Weapons Convention in 2003 on the basis of a civil society draft, was barely heard at the 2010 conference, and no other state expressed awareness of or interest in that draft. A senior Western diplomat has also remarked that it appears that even the strongest supporters of nuclear disarmament (both NAM and non-NAM) today do not in fact believe in its feasibility. The comment was made at a meeting held under Chatham House rules, autumn 2011.

56 See, for example, Working Paper submitted by Germany to the second session of the NPT Preparatory Committee for the 2010 Review Conference, NPT/CONF.2010/PC.II/WP.21, 30 April 2008.

57 The inclusion of existing stocks in the negotiations is the condition that Pakistan has put forward for breaking the deadlock at the Conference on Disarmament, but NAM has not mobilised around this position. Once negotiations start, however, NAM will insist on covering the issue of stocks.

58 A 'new group' does not mean that it will be or has to be completely different from the New Agenda Coalition in terms of membership. However, the NAM–West engagement could very well benefit from the involvement of Norway, Switzerland and Austria, and perhaps new actors from among the non-aligned.

59 The Model Additional Protocol is contained in INFCIRC/540. For a discussion of the origins and content of the AP see John Carlson, 'IAEA Safeguards Additional Protocol', Research Paper commissioned by the International Commission on Nuclear Non-proliferation and Disarmament, January 2009.

60 'Working Paper Submitted by the Members of the Group of Non-Aligned States Parties to the Treaty on the Non-Proliferation of Nuclear Weapons', Recommendation 33, NPT/Conf.2010/WP.46, 28 April 2010.

61 However, even among Middle Eastern states, as demonstrated by the case of the UAE, diversity of views exists.

62 Agreement of 13 December 1991 between the Republic of Argentina, the Federative Republic of Brazil, the Brazilian–Argentine Agency for Accounting and Control of Nuclear Materials (ABACC) and the International Atomic Energy Agency for the Application of Safeguards, http://www.iaea.org/Publications/Documents/Infcircs/Others/inf435.shtml. The agreement is a substitute for a comprehensive safeguards agreement (INFCIRC/153) and allows reliance on the ABACC for verification.

63 For a brief discussion of Brazil's concerns about the Additional Protocol, including industrial espionage and revelation of past activities, see Mark Hibbs, 'Nuclear Suppliers Group and the IAEA Additional Protocol', Nuclear Energy Brief, Carnegie Endowment for International Peace, 18 August 2010, http://www.carnegieendowment. org/publications/index.cfm?fa=view &id=41393.

64 See Yvonne Yew, 'Diplomacy and Nuclear Non-Proliferation: Navigating the Non-Aligned Movement', Discussion Paper no. 2011-07, Harvard Kennedy School, 13 June 2011, p. 8 for a discussion of 'NAM as a Foreign Policy Tool'.

65 Each state that has an Additional Protocol negotiates it with the IAEA individually, but on the basis of the Model Additional Protocol.

66 See paragraph 2.2 of 'Safeguards', working paper submitted by South Africa, NPT/Conf.2000/MCII/WP.1, available at www.reachingcriticalwill. org. This call for all states to adopt the AP, however, was not a call for making it mandatory.

67 'Recommendations to the 2005 NPT Review Conference on strengthening the implementation of articles I, II, III, IV', working paper submitted by the United States, NPT/Conf.2005/PC.III/ WP.19, 30 April 2004.

68 United States statement, Preparatory Committee for the 2005 Review Conference of the Parties to the Treaty on the Non-Proliferation of Nuclear Weapons, NPT/Conf.2005/PC.III/ WP.28, May 2004.

69 See the following Preparatory Committee Working Papers submitted in 2002, 2003 and 2004: NPT/Conf.2005/PC.I/ WP.2, NPT/Conf.2005/PC.II/WP.19, and NPT/Conf.2005/PC.III/WP.24.

70 *Ibid.*

71 See 'Substantive issues to considered by Main Committee II of the 2005 Review Conference of the Parties to the Treaty on the Non-Proliferation of Nuclear Weapons', NPT/Conf.2005/ WP.19, Working Paper submitted by the Non-Aligned States party to the NPT, 2 May 2005, paragraph 10.

72 See NPT/Conf.2010/WP.46, recommendation 32.

73 Sverre Lodgaard, 'NAM and the US–India Nuclear Deal', unpublished essay, James Martin Center for Nonproliferation Studies, Monterey, CA, spring 2010.

74 See 'Statement by Malaysia on behalf of NAM' at the general debate of the 2005 NPT Review Conference, 2 May 2005, and NAM Working Paper on Verification, presented in the general debate by Cuba at the 2007 NPT Prep Com, NPT/conf.2010/PC.1/WP.5 .2, cited by Sverre Lodgaard, 'NAM and the US–India Peaceful Nuclear Cooperation Agreement', unpublished paper, James Martin Center for Nonproliferation Studies, Monterey, CA, 10 February 2010, p. 1.

75 See 'Statement by Malaysia on behalf of NAM', citing statement by Indonesia on behalf of NAM in the general debate of the second Prep Com for the 2010 NPT Review Conference, 28 April 2008.

76 'Statement by H.E. Dr. R.M. Marty M. Natlegawa on behalf of the NAM States Party to the Treaty on the Non-Proliferation of Nuclear Weapons before the 2010 Review Conference of the Parties to the Treaty on the Non-Proliferation of Nuclear Weapons', New York, 3 May 2010, p. 3.

77 See 'Statement on the Islamic Republic of Iran's Nuclear Issue' at the 15th Ministerial Conference of the Non-Aligned Movement, Tehran, Iran, 27–30 July 2008, NAM 2008/Doc.3/Rev.1.

78 Since the IAEA's founding in 1957, its system of safeguards has evolved to take account of nuclear developments, including the diffusion of fuel-fabrication, reprocessing and enrichment facilities. Comprehensive Safeguards Agreements (also referred to as NPT Safeguards) are based on INFCIRC/153.

79 The NAM board members who supported the majority position in favor of the India-specific safeguards agreement included Algeria, Bolivia, Chile, Ecuador, Ethiopia, Ghana, Indonesia, Morocco, Nigeria, Philippines, South Africa and Thailand. Interviews with NAM diplomats, Vienna, summer 2011.

80 This indictment applied with special force to South Africa, which deservingly regards itself as the chief architect and implementation watchdog of the 1995 NPT package of three decisions and one resolution. Accusations of cherry-picking were directed at some NAM members and observers following summit meetings of the India–Brazil–South Africa Dialogue Forum in 2006 and 2007.

81 For a related analysis published shortly after the Rev Con, see William Potter et. al., 'The 2010 NPT Review Conference: Deconstructing Consensus'.

82 At times this group expanded to include representatives from as many as two-dozen countries. Among NAM participants in the group were Brazil, Cuba, Egypt, Iran, Mexico, South Africa and others.

83 Discussed in Potter et al., 'The 2010 NPT Review Conference: Deconstructing Consensus.'

84 On occasions, the group also included diplomats from Argentina, key Arab states, Uruguay (whose permanent representative to the United Nations served as chair of Subsidiary Body 3 at the Rev Con) and other states, as well as representatives of the League of Arab States and the Council of the European Union. See Potter et al, 'The 2010 NPT Review Conference: Deconstructing Consensus'.

85 It is unusual for NAM to delegate members to negotiate on behalf of the group, though an important exception to this tradition occurred in Vienna in September 2010 on the subject of the Israeli Nuclear Capabilities resolution. This case is discussed in more detail in Chapter Three.

86 Conversations with the Review Conference participants, November 2010 and June 2011.

87 'Final Document of the 2010 Review Conference of the States Parties to the Treaty on the Non-Proliferation of Nuclear Weapons', Part I, Conclusions and Recommendations, section IV: The Middle East, particularly 'Implementation of the 1995 Resolution on the Middle East', NPT/Conf.2010/50 (vol. I).

88 Although not discussed in this chapter, one could cite numerous other issues, including the need to reinterpret the withdrawal provisions of Article X of the treaty, the importance to attach to new proliferation challenges such as those posed by non-state actors, and the need to reduce non-strategic nuclear weapons.

89 This explanation was conveyed to one of the authors in interviews

with NAM diplomats in Vienna in summer 2011. On occasion states also may use the common NAM position to promote national policies that otherwise might appear to be too self-serving. As noted earlier, for example, Brazil probably found it convenient to join NAM in its opposition to a mandatory AP rather than to oppose the measure on national grounds related to its domestic enrichment plans.

Chapter Three

1   Mohamed I. Shaker, *The Nuclear Non-Proliferation Treaty*, p. 276.

2   Various parties proposed different formulations/language to be included in Article IV. Nigeria, for example, wanted the article to say that states 'undertake to facilitate' the fullest possible exchange of scientific information (rather than just participate); Italy wanted the addition of materials and equipment, not just information; Mexico's proposal, which served as the basis for paragraph 2 of Article IV, spoke of the states' 'right to participate in the fullest possible exchange of scientific and technological information', whereas the initial text was less specific and did not mention scientific and technological information. See Shaker, *The Nuclear Non-Proliferation Treaty*, vol. I.

3   *Ibid.*, pp. 276–7, 326.

4   Russell Leslie, 'The Good Faith Assumption: Different Paradigmatic Approaches to Non-proliferation Issues', *The Nonproliferation Review*, vol. 18, no. 3, November 2008, p. 483.

5   *Ibid.*

6   Igor Volski, 'Atoms for Peace', *Trud*, 4 July 1954, cited by Arnold Kramish, *Atomic Energy in the Soviet Union* (Stanford, CA: Stanford University Press, 1959), pp. 142–3.

7   See, for example, Algiers Declaration, Fourth Conference of Heads of State or Government of Non-Aligned Countries, Algiers, Algeria, 5–9 September 1973, available at http://www.namegypt.org/en/RelevantDocuments/Pages/default.aspx.

8   Colombo Declaration, Fifth Conference of Heads of State or Government of Non-Aligned Countries, Colombo, Sri Lanka, 16–19 August 1976, available at http://www.namegypt.org/en/RelevantDocuments/Pages/default.aspx.

9   Havana Declaration, 6th Conference of Heads of State or Government of Non-Aligned Countries, Havana, Cuba, 3–9 September 1979, available at http://www.namegypt.org/en/RelevantDocuments/Pages/default.aspx .

10   Shaker, *The Nuclear Non-Proliferation Treaty*, p. 356.

11   The composition of the Board is defined according to Article VI of the IAEA Statute. Thirteen members of the Board are permanent and are designated due to the advanced state of their nuclear industries; 22 members are elected by the General Conference, in accordance with geographic distribution.

12   Although both Brazil and Argentina are always on the board, they alternate

categories of 'designated' and 'elected' members. The composition of the next Board of Governors will be decided at the 2012 General Conference.

13 Havana Declaration, 1979.

14 The decision to create the Vienna Chapter was taken at the NAM Summit in Kuala Lumpur. Iran's initiative was motivated by a desire to engage the movement more directly at the IAEA on issues associated with its nuclear activities. Interviews conducted by one of the authors with several NAM diplomats and officials in Vienna, July–August 2011, including with a senior Iranian diplomat directly involved in the process. An earlier effort to create a NAM chapter in Vienna during the movement's chairmanship by South Africa reportedly was opposed by South Africa, which may have feared that a formal NAM presence at the IAEA might dilute its own influence. Author interviews with officials in Vienna, August 2011.

15 In March 2011, the G-77 for the first time also spoke to the board on the issue of confidentiality related to the Agency's work on verification and safeguards. This development was the direct result of the Iranian chairmanship of the G-77. According to some NAM diplomats, Iran pushed for the action despite the fact that NAM had already decided not to raise the issue, believing that the director general had already begun to address its concerns.

16 Leslie, 'The Good Faith Assumption: Different Paradigmatic Approaches to Non-proliferation Issues', p. 484.

17 The IAEA Statute does not foresee obligatory funding for assistance projects. Article XI.B states that, 'upon request, the Agency may also assist any member or group of members to make arrangements to secure necessary funding from outside sources' to implement assistance projects.

18 NAM states, for their part, tend to discount the substantial contribution made by the United States to the TCF – a pledge of $50 million over five years. On this point, see also Yew, 'Diplomacy and Nuclear Non-Proliferation', p. 16.

19 The Western group dominates the board to such a degree that it need persuade only very few NAM members to join its cause to achieve a majority.

20 'Statement of the Director General', Record of the First Meeting, 47th Session of the IAEA General Conference, 15 September 2003, GOV(47)/OR.1.

21 Mohamed ElBaradei, 'Towards a Safer World', *Economist*, 16 October 2003, available at http://www.iaea. org/newscenter/statements/2003/ ebte20031016.html.

22 The original idea for multinational fuel arrangements can be traced to the Baruch Plan of 1946. The idea was raised again during the negotiation of the NPT and discussed at the first Review Conference in 1975.

23 For a comprehensive review and comparison of the 12 proposals, see Yuri Yudin, *Multilateralization of the Nuclear Fuel Cycle: Assessment of Existing Proposals* (Geneva: United Nations, 2009).

24 Daniel Horner, 'IAEA Board Approves Russian Fuel Bank Plan', *Arms Control Association*, January–February 2010, http://www.armscontrol.org/ act/2010_01-02/FuelBank.

25 'Joint Statement of G-77 and NAM', IAEA Board of Governors, June 24, 2009, http://www.cubaminrex.cu/

english/UNGA/Articulos/63Session/Statements/24-06-09-Joint.html.

26 *Ibid*. Pakistan was in the room but did not participate in the vote and was recorded as ' absent', an indication of its disapproval.

27 'UN Atomic Watchdog Approves Nuclear Fuel Assurance Proposal', AFP, 10 March 2011. The countries that abstained were Argentina, Brazil, Ecuador, Peru, Singapore, South Africa, Tunisia and Venezuela. Pakistan, again, while being in the room, did not take part in the voting.

28 References are to the General Debate and Main Committee III statements by Brazil, Egypt, Malaysia and South Africa. See also South Africa's statement at the Special Event in 2006.

29 See record of the meetings of the 50th Session of the IAEA General Conference, available at http://www.iaea.org/About/Policy/GC/GC50/Records/index.html.

30 Lance Joseph, 'Multilateral Approaches to the Nuclear Fuel Cycle', Issue Brief, Lowe Institute for International Policy, August 2005, p. 7.

31 *Ibid*.

32 One could argue that the first modality, involving government guarantees of supply, fuel-lease and take-back offers, was the least ambitious, but it was also essentially not multilateral in nature. An overview of possible modalities is available in Tariq Rauf, 'Background and Report of the Expert Group on Multilateral Approaches to the Nuclear Fuel Cycle', presented to the conference 'Multilateral, Technical and Organizational Approaches for the Nuclear Fuel Cycle Aimed at Strengthening the Non-Proliferation Regime', Moscow, 13–15 July 2005, available at http://www.iaea.

org/newscenter/news/pdf/rauf_report220605.pdf.

33 Cole Harvey, 'From Theory to Reality: The Evolution of Multilateral Assurance of Nuclear Fuel Supply', Issue Brief, Nuclear Threat Initiative, 24 March 2011.

34 *Ibid*.

35 *Ibid*.

36 'Multinational Fuel Bank Proposal Reaches Key Milestone', Staff Report, International Atomic Energy Agency, Vienna, 6 March 2009, http://www.iaea.org/newscenter/news/2009/fbankmilestone.html

37 Horner, 'IAEA Board Approves Fuel Bank Plan'.

38 GOV/INF/2006/10, June 2006.

39 One such question concerns the fabrication of actual fuel from the LEU, once the need arises. Fuel is normally supplied by the party that constructed the reactor, but the IAEA does not hold licenses for fuel-fabrication, nor does it have any fuel fabrication facility at its disposal. This problem is now being studied by the US Department of Energy, but NAM requests to address this question in the framework of considerations at the IAEA were left unanswered.

40 'President Announces New Measures to Counter the Threat of WMD', The White House, 11 February 2004, http://georgewbush-whitehouse.archives.gov/news/releases/2004/02/20040211-4.html

41 *Ibid*.

42 Writing in the *IAEA Bulletin* about the findings of the Expert Group, Bruno Pellaud asked: 'Are multilateral nuclear approaches an old idea whose time has come?' He answered his own question in the affirmative. The phrase was subsequently used by other

non-proliferation experts in relation to multilateral fuel approaches. Bruno Pellaud, 'Which Way forward for Multilateral Approaches? An International Expert Group Examines Approaches', *IAEA Bulletin*, vol. 46, no. 2, March 2006, pp. 38–40.

43 There is no shortage of literature devoted to Iran's nuclear developments. For a detailed chronology of developments, see the Nuclear Threat Initiative's Nuclear Chronology at http://www.nti. org/e_research/profiles/Iran/Nuclear/ chronology.html; the IAEA has an archive of main events and relevant documents at http://www.iaea.org/ newscenter/focus/iaeairan/iaea_ resolutions.shtml.

44 See, for example, NAM statements on Iran adopted at the Tehran Ministerial Conference in 2008, at the 14th NAM Summit in Havana in 2006, the Ministerial Meeting in Malaysia in 2006, and the NAM Troika Communiqué adopted in Tehran in 2005.

45 See William Potter, 'India and the New Look of US Nonproliferation Policy', *The Nonproliferation Review*, vol. 12, no. 2, July 2005, pp. 343–54.

46 'Declaration of the Meeting of Ministers of Foreign Affairs of the Non-Aligned Movement at the 58th Session of the UN General Assembly', paragraph 12, New York, 23 September 2003, http:// www.un.org/special-rep/ohrlls/ohrlls/ NAM%20at%2058th%20session.htm.

47 'NAM Troika Communiqué', Tehran, Iran, 11 November 2005, http://www.un.int/malaysia/NAM/ Nam11nov2005com.PDF.

48 'Statement on the Islamic Republic of Iran's Nuclear Issue', Ministerial Meeting of the Coordinating Bureau of the Non-Aligned Movement, Putrajaya, Malaysia, 30 May 2006; Statement on the Islamic Republic of Iran's Nuclear Issue, 14th Summit Conference of Heads of State or Government, Havana, 16 September 2006.

49 'Statement on the Islamic Republic of Iran's Nuclear Issue', 15th Ministerial Conference of the Non-Aligned Movement, Tehran, Iran, 27–30 July 2008, contained in INFCIRC/733, http://www.iaea.org/newscenter/ focus/iaeairan/ms_communications. shtml.

50 Excerpts from NAM Vienna Chapter statements concerning Iran, made between September 2003 and August 2005, are cited in INFCIRC/657, Annex II, 15 September 2005.

51 All IAEA Board resolutions on Iran are available at the IAEA website, http:// www.iaea.org/newscenter/focus/ iaeairan/index.shtml.

52 See 'Implementation of NPT Safeguards Agreement in the Islamic Republic of Iran', Resolution of the IAEA Board of Governors, GOV/2005/77, 24 September 2005, operative paragraph 1. Non-compliance in the context of Article XII.C does not equal non-compliance with the NPT. In the case of Iran, it means that there was a failure to fully declare materials and facilities and subsequent failure to take corrective action in response to the director general's and board's requests. IAEA Statute is available at http://www.iaea. org/About/statute_text.html#A1.12.

53 These were Argentina, Ecuador, Ghana, India, Peru and Singapore in September 2005, and Argentina, Brazil, Colombia, Ecuador, Egypt, Singapore, Sri Lanka and Yemen in February 2006.

54 Tanya Ogilvie-White, 'International Responses to Iranian Nuclear Defiance: The Non-Aligned Movement and the Issue of Non-Compliance', *The European Journal of International Law*, vol. 18, no. 3, 2007, pp. 453–76.

55 *Ibid.*, p. 457.

56 *Ibid.*, pp. 468, 474.

57 See Tehran Statement of October 2003; IAEA Director General reports for November 2004 and September 2005, and a special communication of August 2005; all available at http://www.iaea.org/newscenter/focus/iaeairan/index.shtml.

58 'Implementation of NPT Safeguards Agreement in the Islamic Republic of Iran and Related Board Resolutions', Resolution of the IAEA Board of Governors, GOV/2005/64, 11 August 2005.

59 As a consequence of the vote, the Malaysian representative was recalled to Kuala Lumpur and quickly replaced. A few months later, in April 2010, the Malaysian government announced it had stopped the supply of gasoline to Iran because of its nuclear programme. P. Parameswaran, 'Malaysia Warns Iran after Cutting off Gasoline Supplies', AFP, 16 April 2010.

60 Interview with NAM diplomat by one of the authors in Vienna, July 2011.

61 See, for example, Brazil's statement at the Meeting of the NPT Preparatory Committee in 2004, available at www.reachingcriticalwill.org.

62 UN Security Council Resolution 1747, Statement before the Vote, by South Africa, 24 March 2007, http://www.un.org/News/Press/docs/2007/sc8980.doc.htm.

63 UN Security Council Resolution 1803, Statement before the Vote, by South Africa, 3 March 2008, http://www.un.org/News/Press/docs/2008/sc9268.doc.htm.

64 'Implementation of the NPT Safeguards Agreement and Relevant Provisions of Security Council Resolutions in the Islamic Republic of Iran', Annex, Repot by the Director General, GOV/2011/65, November 2011,.

65 As usual, the report appeared first on the website of the Institute for Science and International Security (ISIS), http://isis-online.org/uploads/isis-reports/documents/IAEA_Iran_8Nov2011.pdf.

66 For the full text of Questions and Answers, see 'Iran IAEA Envoy Explains: Realities about Iran's Peaceful Nuclear Program', Fars News Agency, http://english.farsnews.com/newstext.php?nn=9007272711.

67 See the following IAEA General Conference Resolutions: GC(XXXI)/Res/470, GC(XXXII)/Res/487, GC(XXXIII)/Res/506, GC(XXXIV)/Res/526, and GC(XXXV)/Res/570. See also Leslie, 'The Good Faith Assumption', p. 488.

68 'Israeli Nuclear Capabilities and Threat', resolution adopted during the 342nd plenary meeting of the IAEA General Conference, GC(XXXV)/Res/570, 20 September 1991.

69 See record of the 352nd Plenary Meeting of the IAEA General Conference, GC(XXXVI)/OR.352, 25 September 1992, p. 3.

70 *Ibid.* pp. 8–22; also 'Application of IAEA Safeguards in the Middle East', resolution adopted during the 352nd plenary meeting of the IAEA General Conference, GC(XXXVI)/Res/601, 25 September 1992.

71 'Application of IAEA Safeguards in the Middle East', GC(XXXVI)/RES/601.

72 Letter from the Resident Representative of Kuwait to the IAEA, 7 May 1998, contained in GC(42)/8.

73 For example, neither Brazil nor Argentina – both NAM observers – was party to the NPT. India is still not a party. Interestingly, Pakistan, while also an NPT outlier, routinely supports calls for Israel to accede to the treaty.

74 According to Rule 12 of the Rules and Procedures of the General Conference, all 'items the inclusion of which has been decided by the General Conference at a previous session' must be included in the agenda. If no such decision was taken at a previous session on a particular item, a member state or the Board of Governors should propose its inclusion if they wish the GC to consider and/or take action on it.

75 Comments from a NAM diplomat, Monterey, California, June 2011.

76 At the start of the General Conference, an Israeli representative informed the conference president that his delegation would not support the resolution on the IAEA Safeguards in the Middle East if the INC was brought up for discussion. The letter was circulated, and can be found in document GC(50)/28, 21 September 2006.

77 'Arab League Head: Mideast Peace Process "Dead"', CNN, 15 July 2006, http://articles.cnn.com/2006-07-15/world/arab.league_1_israeli-warplanes-hezbollah-militants-arab-league?_s=PM:WORLD.

78 See Gaukhar Mukhatzhanova, Georgia Adams and Jean du Preez, 'UN Disarmament Committee Forecasts Troubled Nonproliferation Future', Issue Brief, Nuclear Threat Initiative, March 2007.

79 Statement by Egypt at the plenary meeting of the IAEA General Conference, 51st session, 2007.

80 Record of the 8th Plenary Meeting, 52nd session of the IAEA General Conference, GC(52)/OR.8, 3 October 2008.

81 Record of the 10th Plenary Meeting, 52nd session of the IAEA General Conference, GC(52)/OR.10, 4 October 2008.

82 Statement by Egypt, Record of the 9th Plenary Meeting, 53rd session of the IAEA General Conference, GC(53)/OR.9, 17 September 2009.

83 Record of the 10th Plenary Meeting of the 53rd session of the IAEA General Conference, GC(53)/OR.10, 18 September 2009.

84 'Israeli Nuclear Capabilities', Resolution adopted during the meeting of the IAEA General Conference, GC(53)/RES/17, 18 September 2009.

85 Record of the 10th Meeting, 54th session of the IAEA General Assembly, GC(54)/OR.9, 24 September 2010.

86 Interview by one of the authors in Vienna, July 2011.

87 Record of the 10th Meeting, 54th session of the IAEA General Assembly, GC(54)/OR.10, 24 September 2010.

88 The European states, in the meantime, referred primarily to the 2010 Rev Con and progress on the NWFZ. Record of the 10th Meeting, 54th session of the IAEA General Assembly, GC(54)/OR.10, 24 September 2010.

89 Conversation with a NAM diplomat, Vienna, summer 2011.

90 Conversations with NAM diplomats, Vienna and New York, autumn 2011.

91 The authors have attended many international conferences, including those hosted at the United Nations, where professional interpreters confused the translation.

92 For a discussion of different forms that nuclear terrorism can take, see Charles

Ferguson and William Potter, *The Four Faces of Nuclear Terrorism* (New York: Routledge, 2005). This reorientation in thinking is highlighted in the statement by IAEA Director General Mohamed ElBaradei in a 1 November 2001 IAEA Press Release. See 'IAEA on Threat of Nuclear Terrorism' at http:/www. iwar.org.uk/cyberterror/resources/ nke/11/11-05001.htm. See also his speech on 'Nuclear Proliferation and the Potential Threat of Nuclear Terrorism', Asia-Pacific Nuclear Safeguards and Security Conference, Sydney, Australia, 8 November 2004 at http://www.iaea.org/newscenter/ statements/3004/ebsp2004m013.html.

93 The IAEA issued its first set of 'Recommendations for the Physical Protection of Nuclear Material' in June 1972. The agency director general also circulated a draft 'Convention on Physical Protection of Nuclear Facilities, Material, and Transports' to IAEA member states, which led to the adoption of the Convention on the Physical Protection of Nuclear Material in 1979 and the convention's entry into force in 1980. For a discussion of IAEA activities in the nuclear security sector see Jack Boureston and Andrew Semmel, 'The IAEA and Nuclear Security: Trends and Prospects', Policy Analysis Brief, The Stanley Foundation, December 2010.

94 'IAEA Board of Governors approves IAEA Action Plan to combat nuclear terrorism', IAEA press release, 19 March 2002. The board has never formally approved the action plan, but the agency has acted consistent with the plan. Interview by one of the authors with senior IAEA official, August 2011.

95 Former IAEA Director General Mohamed ElBaradei frequently compared the Khan network to a 'nuclear Wal-Mart'.

96 See Boureston and Andrew Semmel, 'The IAEA and Nuclear Security', pp. 3–4, for a discussion of many of these activities.

97 Interviews by one of the authors with NAM diplomats and IAEA officials, July–August 2011. The NAM Vienna Chapter has provided input on the issue of nuclear safety and security to the NPT review process on at least one occasion. In spring 2009, in advance of the 2009 NPT Prep Com, it emphasised that 'while nuclear safety and security are national responsibilities, the development of international safety standards and nuclear security norms, based on best practices, should be a key IAEA role'. It also added that 'nuclear safety and security considerations should not be used to hamper the peaceful utilization of nuclear energy, especially in developing countries'. See, 'Draft Input of the NAM Vienna Chapter for the Third Session of the Preparatory Committee for the 2010 Review Conference of the Parties to the NPT', 9 April 2009.

98 Final Document of the 13th Conference of Heads of State or Government of the Non-Aligned Movement, Kuala Lumpur, Malaysia, 24 February 2003, paragraph 89. This reference to the need to strengthen the physical protection of radioactive material appears to be the first instance in which nuclear security is addressed in a NAM summit document.

99 See, for example, support for UN General Assembly Resolution 60/78 in paragraph 105 of the Final Document of the 14th Conference of Heads of State or Government of the Non-

Aligned Movement, Havana, Cuba, 16 September 2006.

100 The Havana Summit Final Document, for example, 'while noting the adoption of Resolution 1540 (2004) and Resolution 1673 (2006) by the Security Council', underlines the need to ensure that any action by the Security Council does not undermine the UN Charter, existing multilateral treaties on weapons of mass destruction, or the role of the General Assembly (paragraph 105). Similar language appears in paragraph 47 of the Final Document of the 15th NAM Summit in Sharm El-Sheikh, Egypt, 11–16 July 2009.

101 Interestingly, some states, including Iran, appeared to have preferred the idea of adding a new major programme to the agency's structure rather than attempting to fit nuclear security/terrorism work into the existing set of agency programmes. This approach may have been viewed as a way to prevent the diversion of funds from other projects within existing programmes.

102 The only NAM member with a substantial quantity of fissile material is South Africa, which has a large stock of HEU, a remnant of its former weapons programme.

103 See Letter of 27 October 2009 to Director General Mohamed ElBaradei from the Ambassador of Egypt on behalf of the Vienna Chapter of the Non-Aligned Movement, which appears as IAEA INFCIRC/772, 5 November 2009. NAM members and observers on the board at the time included Burkina Faso, Costa Rica, Libya, Mexico, Uganda and Vietnam. Although the Egyptian chair sent the letter on behalf of NAM, it required five meetings of NAM before agreement could be reached on

the letter, and a number of members expressed major reservations.

104 At least one NAM member sought to include reference to HEU minimisation in the letter, but did not insist on the matter after meeting resistance from other NAM members who were supportive of that particular activity. Interview with senior NAM official involved in the NAM debate over 1887, Vienna, August 2011.

105 The Vienna letter appears to have pre-empted a response by the New York Coordinating Bureau, which was unable to achieve consensus on a strong response. One of the authors has observed heated exchanges between NAM members over the issue of the Vienna Chapter's action.

106 For an extended discussion of the international politics of HEU minimisation, see William C. Potter, 'Nuclear Terrorism and the Global Politics of HEU Elimination', in William C. Potter and Cristina Hansell (eds), The Global Politics of Combatting Nuclear Terrorism: A Supply-Side Approach (New York: Routledge, 2010), pp. 7–30.

107 The major impact of the HEU initiative, if implemented, would be to reduce the HEU holdings of the United States and Russia, which possess by far the largest stockpiles of HEU in the civilian sector.

108 For a more detailed analysis of the Norwegian symposium see Cristina Chuen and William Potter, 'The Oslo Symposium: On the Road to HEU Minimization', James Martin Center for Nonproliferation Studies, 22 August 2006, at cns.miis.edu/pubs/week/0060822.htm.

109 The relevant language in the 2009 resolution 'Calls upon all States to

manage responsibly and minimize to the greatest extent that is technically and economically feasible the use of highly enriched uranium for civilian purposes, including by working to convert research reactors and radioisotope production processes to the use of low enriched uranium fuels and targets.'

110 NAM members and observers made up more than 40% of the countries that participated in the summit.

111 It is probably not coincidental that the change in the South African position on HEU minimisation coincided with its conversion of the SAFARI-1 reactor to LEU fuel. The conversion of the reactor that produces radioisotopes, including Mo-99, was completed in 2009. 'South African Radioisotope Production on Target', *World Nuclear News*, 17 September 2010, http://www. world-nuclear-news.org/RS-South_

African_radioisotope_production_on_target-1709107.html.

112 Their support for the process is probably the result of their being part of it. Some NAM states, however, continue to criticise the process by which new, limited-membership negotiating bodies are created, and may seek to forge a common NAM position that advocates a halt to nuclear summits following the one in Seoul. Interviews in Vienna, July–August 2011.

113 See Ray Acheson, 'Repot on the High Level Meeting on Nuclear Safety and Security', Reaching Critical Will, 22 September, 2011, http://www. reachingcriticalwill.org/political/ energy/hlm/RCW-report.html.

114 Lawrence Scheinman, *The International Atomic Energy Agency and the World Nuclear Order*, (Washington DC: RFF Press, 1987), pp. 209, 218–25.

115 *Ibid.*, p. 214.

Chapter Four

1 The anniversary has generated its own debate within the movement as to the appropriate venue for commemoration of the occasion. Some NAM members were reluctant to have an observer (Serbia) host the formal event. The issue was resolved by convening two high-level meetings during the year – the 'Main Commemorative Event' in Bali, Indonesia, in May 2011 and a second meeting of former chairs of the Movement in Belgrade, Serbia, during the first week of September 2011. See 'Bali Commemorative Declaration on the 50th Anniversary of the

Establishment of the Non-Aligned Movement', NAM 2011/Doc7/Rev.1. For an account of the Belgrade meeting, see 'Non-aligned Movement celebrates 50th anniversary in Belgrade', Xinhua, http://news. xinhuanet.com/english2010/ world/2011-09/06/c_131100906.htm.

2 See 'Bali Commemorative Declaration', p. 2, first bullet point.

3 Final Document, 16th Ministerial Conference and Commemorative Meeting of the Non-Aligned Movement, Bali, Indonesia, 23–27 May 2011, pp. 61–2, paragraphs 171–5.

4 *Ibid.*, p. 54, paragraph 136.

5 Russell Leslie, 'The Good Faith Assumption: Different Paradigmatic Approaches to Nonproliferation Issues', *The Nonproliferation Review*, vol. 18, no. 3, November 2008, p. 480. In support of this assertion, he cites the Final Document of the 13th ministerial conference of the Movement of Non-Aligned Countries, Cartagena, Colombia, April 8–9, 2000.

6 *Ibid.*, pp. 480–1.

7 NAM has developed a number of formulas in its declarations as a means to finesse the issue of double standards. These typically involve reference to the need for nuclear-weapon states (NWS) to disarm 'in accordance with their relevant multilateral legal obligations'. As India and Pakistan are neither NWS according to the NPT definition nor parties to the NPT or other multilateral treaties that commit them to nuclear disarmament, they can maintain the façade that the declarations do not apply to them.

8 At India's urging, NAM statements related to disarmament typically have been directed at the shortcomings of NPT states, a not very subtle means of deflecting attention from the three NAM nuclear-weapons possessors. For similar reasons, recent NAM declarations also tend to eschew a focus on the need for immediate and concrete disarmament measures that would impact some of its own members in favour of a discussion of the desired end-state of a nuclear-free world. The authors are unaware of any NAM pronouncements that are critical of North Korea's nuclear tests.

9 See, for example, the Nuclear Suppliers Group deliberations in June 2011; Fredrick Dahl, 'Nuclear Suppliers Tighten Trade Rules, May Irk India', Reuters, 28 June 2011; and Siddharth Varadarajan, 'NSG Ends India's "Clean" Waiver', *The Hindu*, 25 June 2011.

10 Yvonne Yew, a former diplomat from Singapore, argues that this already is the case and that the movement's collective statements are of limited utility in predicting how individual NAM members will behave on nuclear non-proliferation matters. See Yew, 'Diplomacy and Nuclear Non-Proliferation', p. 4.

11 This point was conveyed to the authors repeatedly by NAM diplomats of very different political persuasions.

12 This concept and its continuing relevance is expressed clearly in paragraph 14 of the 2011 NAM Ministerial Declaration in Bali, p. 8. NAM solidarity on issues involving economic harm rarely translates into concrete financial support for the aggrieved party but rather general support from the collective opposing economic sanctions, the negative effects of globalisation and inequitable global trade.

13 Yew, 'Diplomacy and Nuclear Non-Proliferation', p. 7.

14 Signham and =Hune, *Non-Alignment in an Age of Alignments*, p. 44.

15 These issues are discussed in detail in Singham and Hune, *Non-Alignment in an Age of Alignments*, Chapters 7 and 8.

16 *Ibid.*, p. 46.

17 *Ibid.*, p. 175.

18 These countries were the Central African Empire, Gabon, Kampuchea, Oman, Saudi Arabia, Somalia and Zaire. See *ibid.* pp. 191–2.

19 *Ibid.*, p. 203.

20 See *Ibid.*, pp. 210–32; and Peter Willets, *The Non-Aligned in Havana* (New York: St. Martin's Press, 1981).

21 As noted in Chapter Four, NAM summit and ministerial meetings historically have generated statements of support for Iran's nuclear programme.

22 This tendency is apt to get stronger the more other NAM members hesitate to challenge Iran in its confrontation with the agency. NAM's response to the restricted report for the November 2011 Board of Governors meeting, which was leaked almost immediately, suggests that while some NAM members are troubled by the report's substantive findings, most are sympathetic to the view that the agency acted improperly, or at least imprudently, in terms of the timing of the report and the manner in which it was disseminated. They are particularly upset about charges that the report and briefings related to it may have been provided in advance to some countries but not others.

23 Interviews conducted in spring and summer 2011 in Monterey, CA, and Vienna.

24 The former chief of Iran's Atomic Energy Agency (AEOI), Golamreza Aghazadeh, who is reportedly close to former president Hashemi Rafsanjani, resigned shortly after the disputed presidential elections in 2009. The current head of AEOI, Fereydoon Abbasi-Davani, rose from within the Iranian nuclear establishment and is viewed as more conservative and ideological than the technocrat Aghazadeh. On the other hand, Ali Akbar Salehi, appointed by Ahmadinejad as foreign minister after the abrupt dismissal of Manouchehr Mottaki, is described by some commentators as moderate and pragmatic. See, for example, Mehrzad Boroujerdi, 'Iran's New Foreign Minister: Ali Akbar Salehi', *Tehran Bureau*, 31 January, 2011, http://www.pbs.org/wgbh/pages/frontline/tehranbureau/2011/01/irans-new-foreign-minister-ali-akbar-salehi.html.

25 The deal negotiated between Iran and the 'Vienna Group' (P-5 and the IAEA) in autumn 2009 envisaged the shipment of 1,200kg of Iran's low-enriched uranium to Russia and the supply by France of 120kg of nuclear fuel enriched to 19.75% U-235 for the Tehran Research Reactor. The preliminary agreement was criticised in Iran by both conservative and moderate figures opposed to President Ahmadinejad.

26 Interviews conducted in Vienna in spring and summer 2011.

27 A senior Iranian diplomat acknowledged the possible appearance of manipulation of the chairmanship, but sought to explain the manoeuvre on the basis that the G-77 historically dealt with agency budgetary matters and the issue of safeguards confidentiality involved personnel expenses associated with the agency's use of so-called 'cost-free' experts in the Department of Safeguards. Interview in Vienna, August 2011.

28 On 14 October 2011, Jaakko Laajava, Finnish under-secretary of state, was appointed as facilitator for the 2012 Middle East Conference, while Finland was designated as the host government for the conference.

29 The urgency that NAM attaches to implementation of the 2010 NPT Rev Con recommendations on the Middle East is conveyed in the May 2011 Bali Ministerial Final Document. See p. 60, paragraph 167.

Conclusion

1   A similar point is made by Yvonne Yew, 'Diplomacy and Nuclear Non-Proliferation: Navigating the Non-Aligned Movement', Discussion Paper no. 2011-07, Harvard Kennedy School, 13 June 2011, p. 9.

2   NAM has yet to endorse UNSCR 1540 and the 2009 Summit Declaration reference to it is less than positive, but an increasing number of NAM states are acting in accordance with its mandate. Among NAM members and observers at the Nuclear Security Summit were Algeria, Argentina, Brazil, Chile, Egypt, India, Indonesia, Jordan, Kazakhstan, Malaysia, Mexico, Morocco, Nigeria, Pakistan, Philippines, Saudi Arabia, Singapore, South Africa, Thailand, Ukraine, the UAE and Vietnam. Perhaps most striking was the readiness of key NAM Arab states to participate alongside Israel.

3   This initiative was launched in July 1995 in an effort to promote consensus after the divisive 2005 NPT Review Conference. Members included Australia, Chile, Indonesia, Norway, Romania, South Africa and the United Kingdom. Although the coalition met periodically it played a very limited role in disarmament and non-proliferation and was not engaged in the NPT review process.

4   The group is composed of Australia, Canada, Chile, Germany, Japan, Mexico, the Netherlands, Poland, Turkey and the UAE.

5   Recently, a number of major US foundations have launched training programmes designed to build non-proliferation capacity in developing countries. They include the Carnegie Corporation of New York and the MacArthur Foundation.

Adelphi books are published eight times a year by Routledge Journals, an imprint of Taylor & Francis, 4 Park Square, Milton Park, Abingdon, Oxfordshire OX14 4RN, UK.

A subscription to the institution print edition, ISSN 1944-5571, includes free access for any number of concurrent users across a local area network to the online edition, ISSN 1944-558X

2012 Annual Adelphi Subscription Rates			
Institution	£525	$924 USD	€777
Individual	£239	$407 USD	€324
Online only	£473	$832 USD	€699

Dollar rates apply to subscribers outside Europe. Euro rates apply to all subscribers in Europe except the UK and the Republic of Ireland where the pound sterling price applies. All subscriptions are payable in advance and all rates include postage. Journals are sent by air to the USA, Canada, Mexico, India, Japan and Australasia. Subscriptions are entered on an annual basis, i.e. January to December. Payment may be made by sterling cheque, dollar cheque, international money order, National Giro, or credit card (Amex, Visa, Mastercard).

For more information, visit our website: **http://www.informaworld.com/ adelphipapers.**

For a complete and up-to-date guide to Taylor & Francis journals and books publishing programmes, and details of advertising in our journals, visit our website: **http://www.informaworld.com.**

Ordering information:

USA/Canada: Taylor & Francis Inc., Journals Department, 325 Chestnut Street, 8th Floor, Philadelphia, PA 19106, USA. **UK/Europe/Rest of World:** Routledge Journals, T&F Customer Services, T&F Informa UK Ltd., Sheepen Place, Colchester, Essex, CO3 3LP, UK.

Advertising enquiries to:

USA/Canada: The Advertising Manager, Taylor & Francis Inc., 325 Chestnut Street, 8th Floor, Philadelphia, PA 19106, USA. Tel: +1 (800) 354 1420. Fax: +1 (215) 625 2940.

UK/Europe/Rest of World: The Advertising Manager, Routledge Journals, Taylor & Francis, 4 Park Square, Milton Park, Abingdon, Oxfordshire OX14 4RN, UK. Tel: +44 (0) 20 7017 6000. Fax: +44 (0) 20 7017 6336.